THE
GREAT AMERICAN
COUNTRY SONGBOOK

ISBN 978-0-634-02233-3

HAL•LEONARD®
CORPORATION
7777 W. BLUEMOUND RD. P.O. BOX 13819 MILWAUKEE, WI 53213

Visit Hal Leonard Online at
www.halleonard.com

STRUM AND PICK PATTERNS

This chart contains the suggested strum and pick patterns that are referred to by number at the beginning of each song in this book. The symbols ⊓ and ∨ in the strum patterns refer to down and up strokes, respectively. The letters in the pick patterns indicate which right-hand fingers plays which strings.

p = thumb
i = index finger
m = middle finger
a = ring finger

For example; Pick Pattern 2
is played: thumb - index - middle - ring

Strum Patterns   ## Pick Patterns

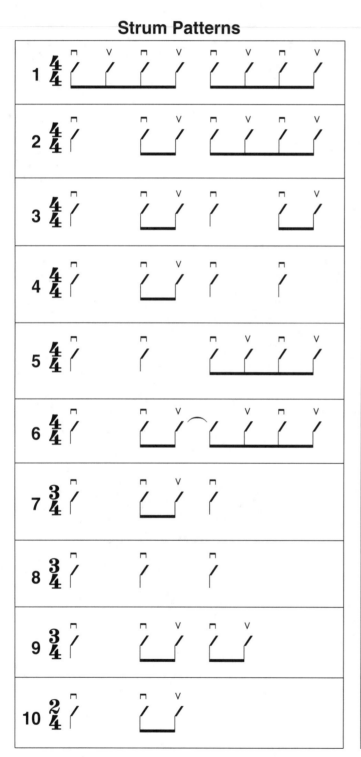
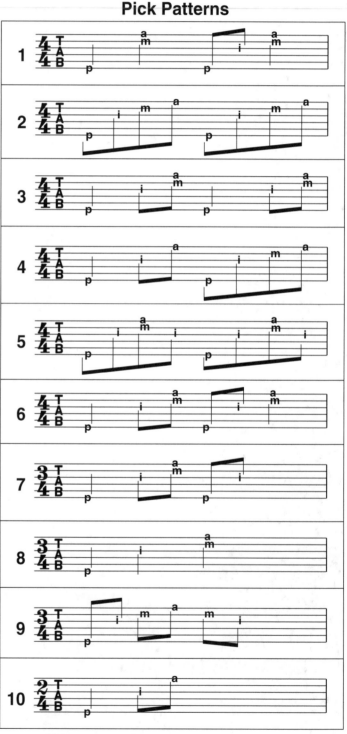

You can use the 3/4 Strum or Pick Patterns in songs written in compound meter (6/8, 9/8, 12/8, etc.).
For example, you can accompany a song in 6/8 by playing the 3/4 pattern twice in each measure.
The 4/4 Strum and Pick Patterns can be used for songs written in cut time (¢) by doubling the note time values in the patterns. Each pattern would therefore last two measures in cut time.

CONTENTS

Act Naturally

Words and Music by Vonie Morrison and Johnny Russell

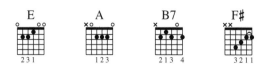

Strum Pattern: 1, 3
Pick Pattern: 2, 4

Verse

Moderately

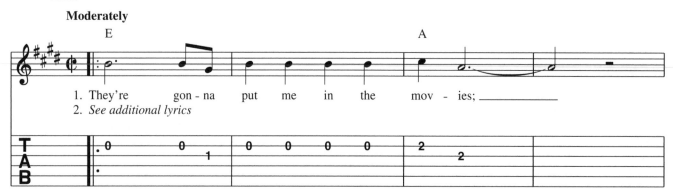

1. They're gon - na put me in the mov - ies; _____
2. *See additional lyrics*

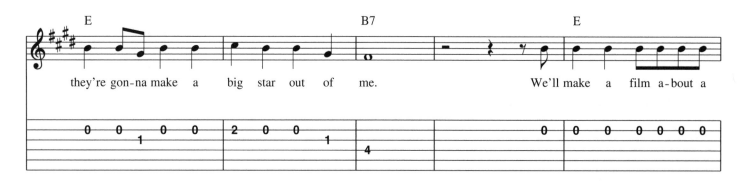

they're gon-na make a big star out of me. We'll make a film a-bout a

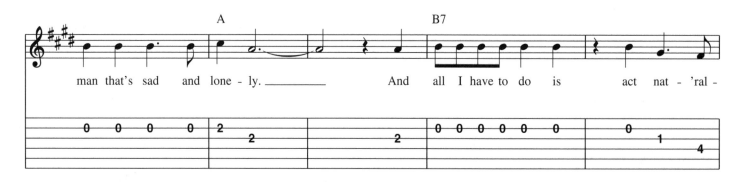

man that's sad and lone - ly. _____ And all I have to do is act nat - 'ral -

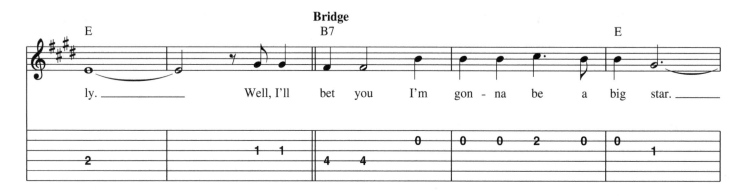

Bridge

ly. _____ Well, I'll bet you I'm gon - na be a big star. _____

Outro

Additional Lyrics

2. We'll make the scene about a man that's sad and lonely,
And beggin' down upon his bended knee.
I'll play the part, but I won't need rehearsin'.
All I have to do is act naturally.

All My Ex's Live in Texas

Words and Music by Lyndia J. Shafer and Sanger D. Shafer

Strum Pattern: 2, 4
Pick Pattern: 2, 4

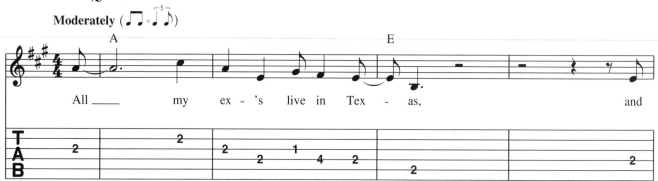

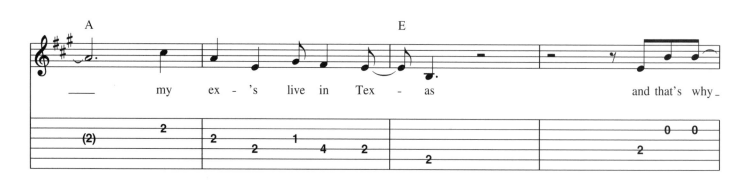

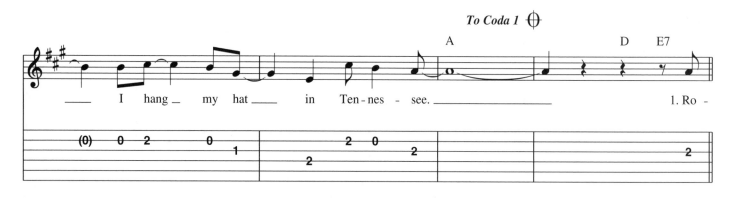

Chorus

my ex - 's live in Tex - as, _and_

_Tex - as is a place __ I'd __ dear-ly love to be. __ But all __ my_

ex - 's live in Tex - as; _there-fore __ I re - side __ in Ten-nes - see. ___

Some folks think I'm hid - ing. _It's been ru-mored that_

I died. _But I'm a-live and well __ in Ten-nes - see. _____

Additional Lyrics

2. I remember that old Frio River
   Where I learned to swim.
   And it brings to mind another time
   Where I wore my welcome thin.
   By transcendental meditation
   I go there each night.
   But I always come back to myself
   Long before daylight.

8

Boot Scootin' Boogie

Words and Music by Ronnie Dunn

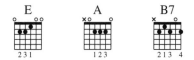

Strum Pattern: 6
Pick Pattern: 3

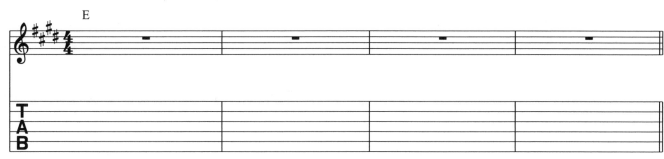

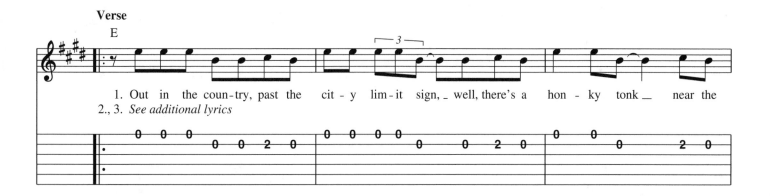

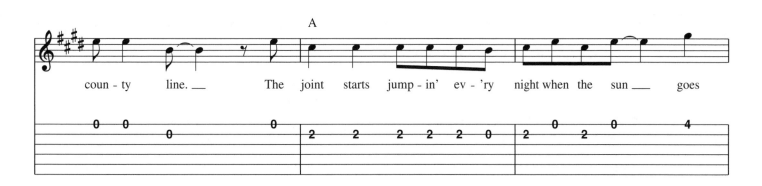

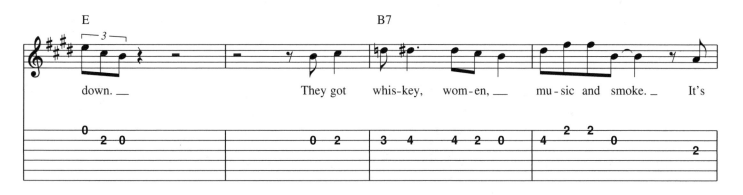

Additional Lyrics

2. I've got a good job, I work hard for my money.
   When it's quittin' time, I hit the door runnin'.
   I fire up my pickup truck and let the horses run.
   I go flyin' down that highway to that hideaway,
   Stuck out in the woods, to do the boot scootin' boogie.

3. The bartender asks me, says, "Son, what will it be?"
   I want a shot at that red-head yonder lookin' at me.
   The dance floor's hoppin' and it's hotter than the Fourth of July.
   I see outlaws, in-laws, crooks and straights,
   All makin' it shake doin' the boot scootin' boogie.

Blue Eyes Crying in the Rain

Words and Music by Fred Rose

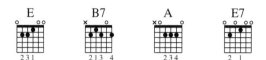

Strum Pattern: 3
Pick Pattern: 4

Verse

Moderately slow

1. In the twi - light glow I see her _____
2. *See additional lyrics*

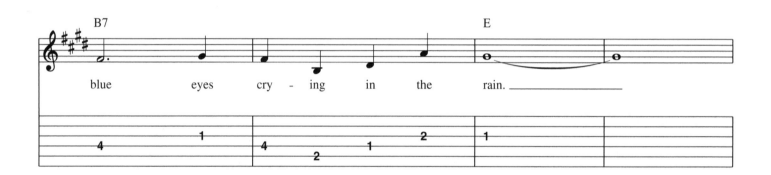

blue eyes cry - ing in the rain. _____

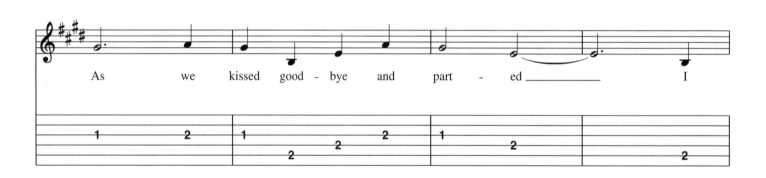

As we kissed good - bye and part - ed _____ I

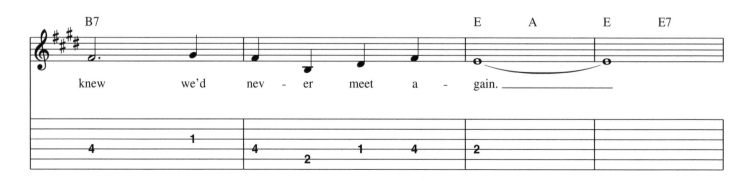

knew we'd nev - er meet a - gain. _____

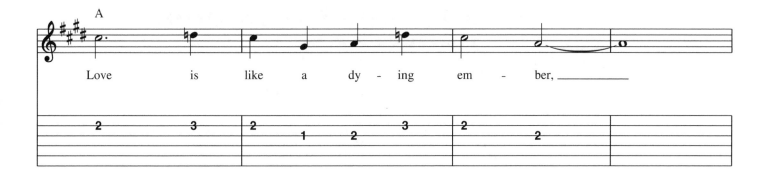

Love   is   like   a   dy - ing   em -   ber, _____

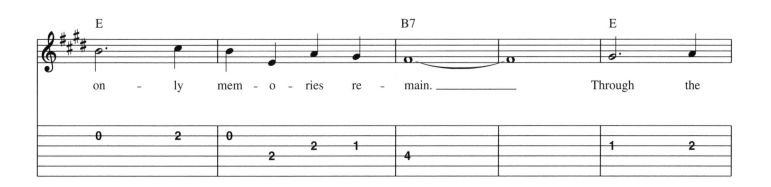

on - ly   mem - o - ries   re - main. _____   Through   the

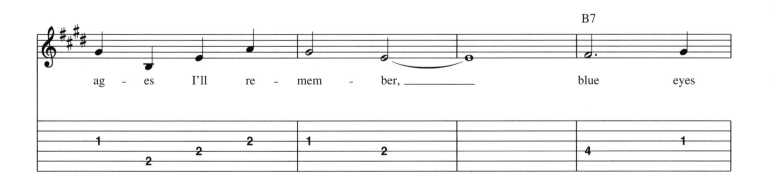

ag - es   I'll   re - mem - ber, _____   blue   eyes

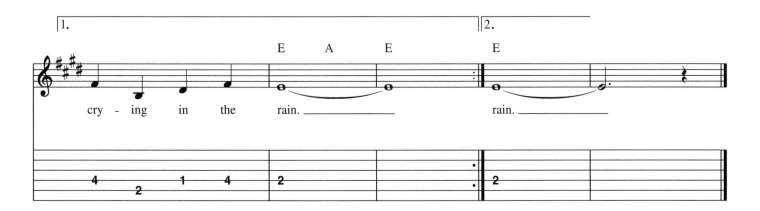

1.
cry - ing   in   the   rain. _____

2.
rain. _____

Additional Lyrics

2. Now my hair has turned to silver,
All my life I've loved in vain.
I can see her star in heaven,
Blue eyes crying in the rain.
Someday when we meet up yonder,
We'll stroll hand in hand again.
In a land that knows no parting,
Blue eyes crying in the rain.

By the Time I Get to Phoenix

Words and Music by Jimmy Webb

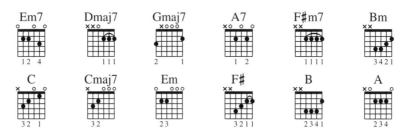

Strum Pattern: 3, 4
Pick Pattern: 3, 4

𝄋 *Verse*

Moderately

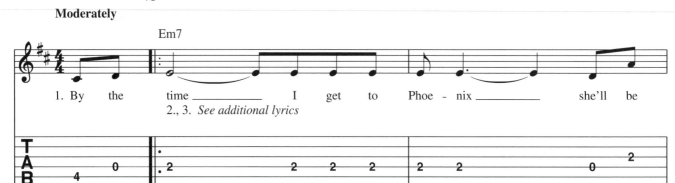

1. By the time _____ I get to Phoe - nix _____ she'll be
2., 3. *See additional lyrics*

ris - in'. _____ She'll find the note I left hang - in' _____ on her

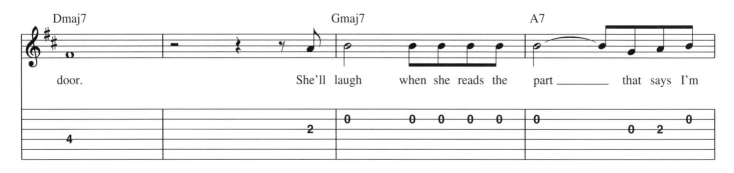

door. She'll laugh when she reads the part _____ that says I'm

To Coda ⊕ |1.

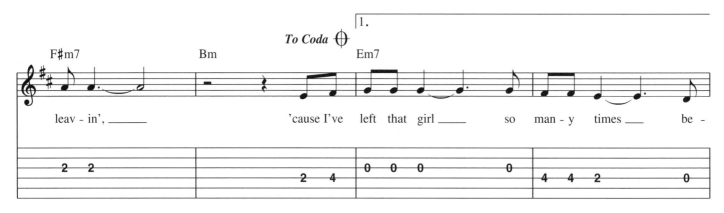

leav - in', _____ 'cause I've left that girl _____ so man - y times _____ be -

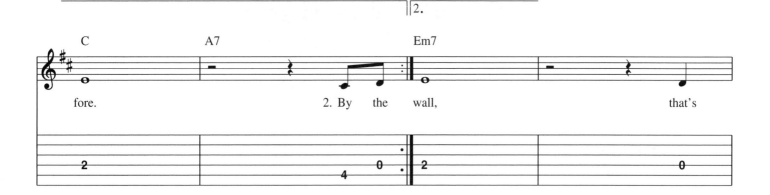

fore.   2. By   the   wall,   that's

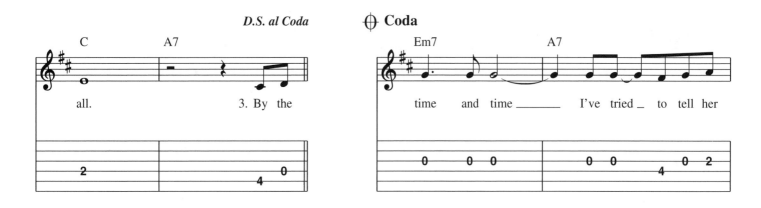

D.S. al Coda   **⊕ Coda**

all.   3. By the   time   and   time _____ I've tried _ to tell her

Outro

so.   She   just   did - n't   know, _____ I   would real - ly

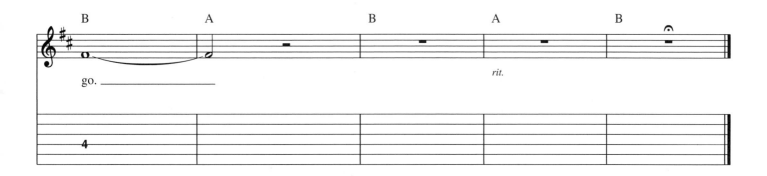

go. _____   *rit.*

Additional Lyrics

2. By the time I make Albuquerque she'll be workin'.
   She'll probably stop at lunch and give a call.
   But she'll just hear that phone keep ringin' off the wall.

3. By the time I make Oklahoma she'll be sleepin'.
   She'll turn softly and call my name out low.
   And she'll cry just to think I'd really leave her,
   Though time and time I've tried to tell her so.

15

Chattahoochee

Words and Music by Jim McBride and Alan Jackson

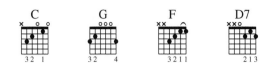

Strum Pattern: 6
Pick Pattern: 3

Verse

Bright Country

1. Way down yon-der on the Chat-ta-hoo-chee it gets hot-ter than a
2. *See additional lyrics*

hoo - chie coo - chie. We laid rub - ber on the Geor - gia as - phalt.

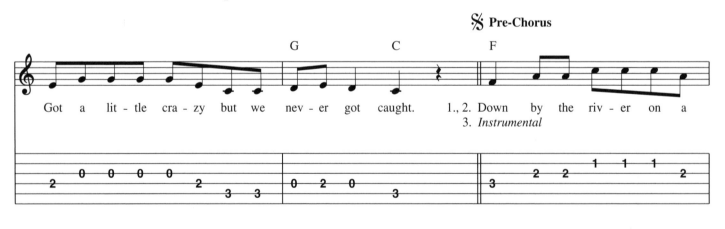

Got a lit-tle cra-zy but we nev-er got caught. 1., 2. Down by the riv-er on a
3. *Instrumental*

Pre-Chorus

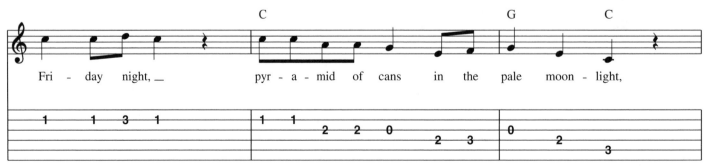

Fri - day night, __ pyr - a - mid of cans in the pale moon - light,

Additional Lyrics

2. Well, we fogged up the windows in my old Chevy;
   I was willin' but she wasn't ready.
   So I settled for a burger and a grape sno-cone.
   I dropped her off early but I didn't go home.

Family Tradition

Words and Music by Hank Williams, Jr.

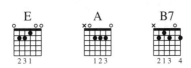

Strum Pattern: 4
Pick Pattern: 3

Verse

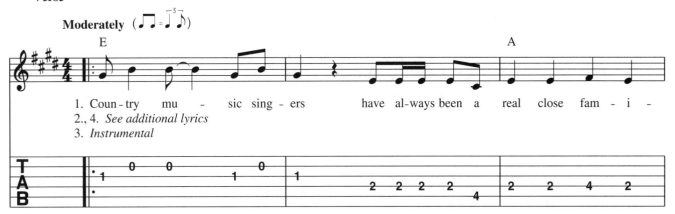

1. Coun - try mu - sic sing - ers have al - ways been a real close fam - i -
2., 4. *See additional lyrics*
3. *Instrumental*

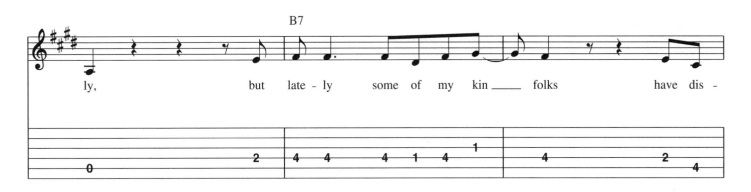

ly, but late - ly some of my kin ____ folks have dis -

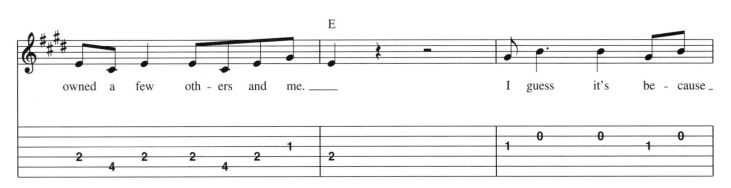

owned a few oth - ers and me. ____ I guess it's be - cause ____

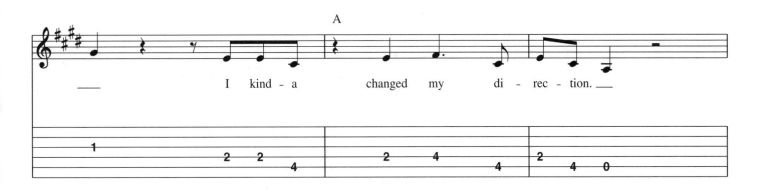

____ I kind - a changed my di - rec - tion. ____

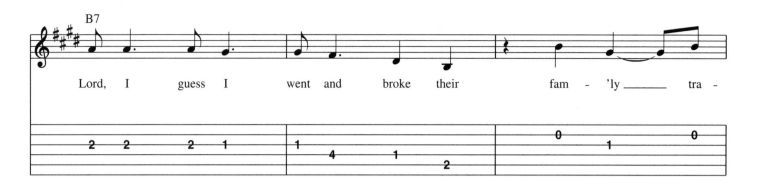

Lord, I guess I went and broke their fam - 'ly ____ tra -

To Coda 1 ⊕   **Chorus**

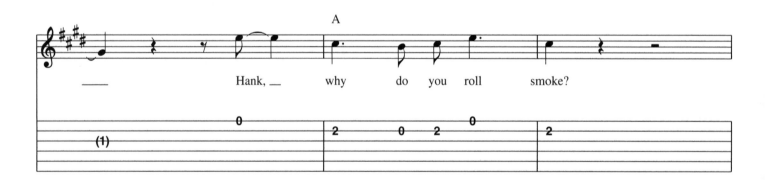

di - tion.

1. They get on me, want to know Hank,   1. Why do you drink?
2., 3. So don't ask me Hank,   2., 3. *See additional lyrics*

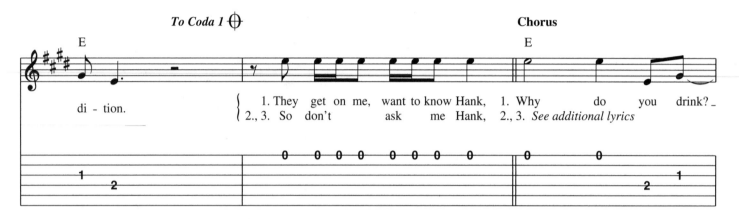

Hank, __ why do you roll smoke?

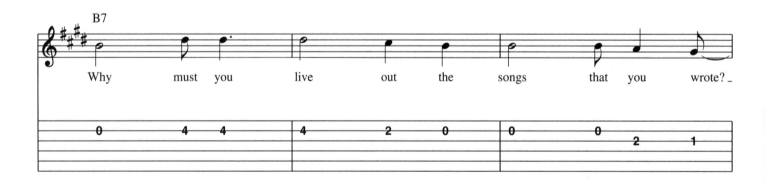

Why must you live out the songs that you wrote? _

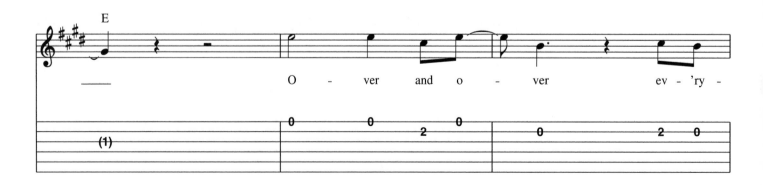

O - ver and o - ver ev - 'ry -

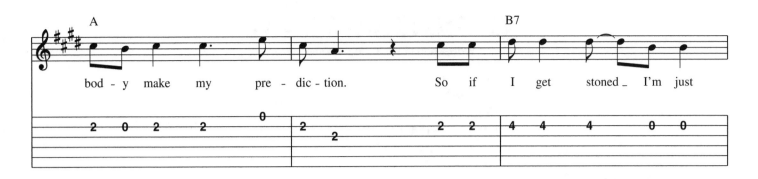

bod - y make my pre - dic - tion. So if I get stoned _ I'm just

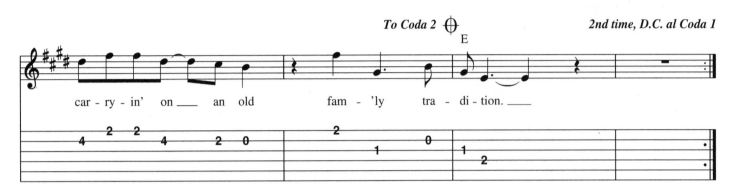

To Coda 2 ⊕

2nd time, D.C. al Coda 1

car - ry - in' on __ an old fam - 'ly tra - di - tion. ____

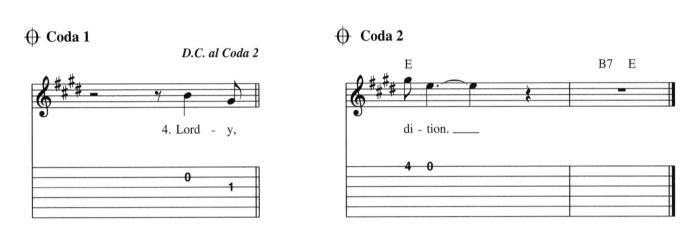

⊕ **Coda 1**

D.C. al Coda 2

4. Lord - y,

⊕ **Coda 2**

di - tion. ____

Additional Lyrics

2. I am very proud of my daddy's name.
   Although his kind of music and mine ain't exactly the same.
   Stop and think it over; put yourself in my position.
   If I get stoned and sing all night long, it's a fam'ly tradition.

Chorus 2. So don't ask me Hank.
   Why do you drink?
   Hank, why do you roll smoke?
   Why must you live out the songs that you wrote?
   If I'm down in a honky tonk, some old slicks tryin' to give me friction,
   I say leave me alone, I'm singin' all night long, it's a fam'ly tradition.

4. Lordy, I have loved some ladies and I have loved Jim Beam.
   And they both tried to kill me in Nineteen Seventy Three.
   When that doctor asked me, "Son, how'd you get in this condition?"
   I said, "Hey, Saw Bones, I'm just carryin' on an old fam'ly tradition.

Chorus 3. So don't ask me Hank.
   Why do you drink?
   Hank, why do you roll smoke?
   Why must you live out the songs that you wrote?
   Stop and think it over, try to put yourself in my unique position.
   If I get stoned and sing all night long, it's a fam'ly tradition.

Cold, Cold Heart

Words and Music by Hank Williams

Verse

oth - er love be - fore my time made your heart sad and blue. And

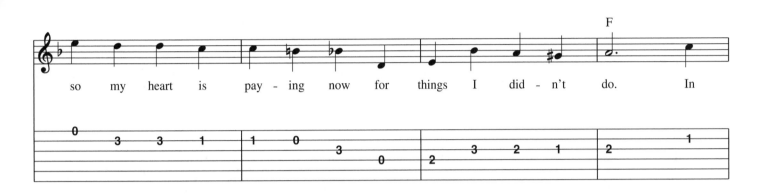

so my heart is pay - ing now for things I did - n't do. In

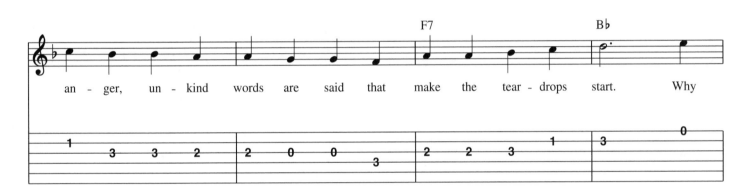

an - ger, un - kind words are said that make the tear - drops start. Why

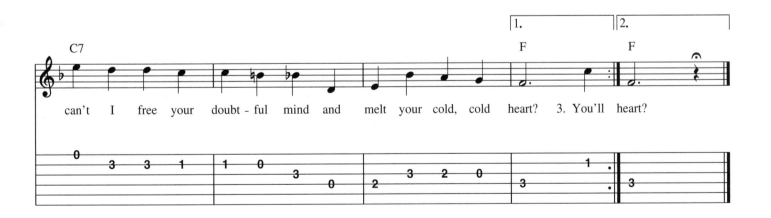

can't I free your doubt - ful mind and melt your cold, cold heart? 3. You'll heart?

Additional Lyrics

3. You'll never know how much it hurts
   To see you sit and cry.
   You know you need and want my love
   Yet you're afraid to try.
   Why do you run and hide from life?
   To try it just ain't smart.
   Why can't I free your doubtful mind
   And melt your cold, cold heart?

4. There was a time when I believed
   That you belong to me.
   But now I know your heart is shackled
   To a memory.
   The more I learn to care for you,
   The more we drift apart.
   Why can't I free your doubtful mind
   And melt your cold, cold heart?

Could I Have This Dance

from URBAN COWBOY

Words and Music by Wayland Holyfield and Bob House

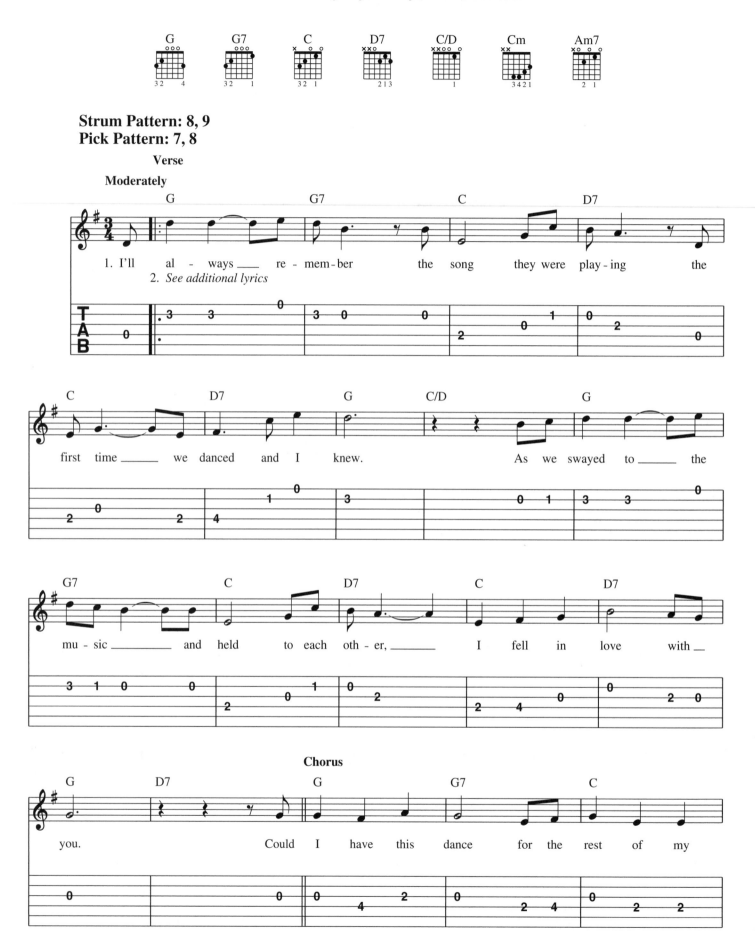

Strum Pattern: 8, 9
Pick Pattern: 7, 8

Additional Lyrics

2. I'll always remember that magic moment,
   When I held you close to me.
   As we moved together, I knew forever,
   You're all I'll ever need.

Crazy

Words and Music by Willie Nelson

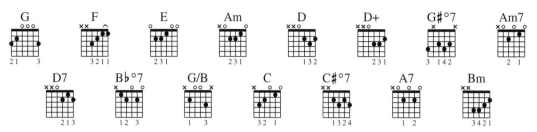

Strum Pattern: 4
Pick Pattern: 3

Verse

Moderately slow

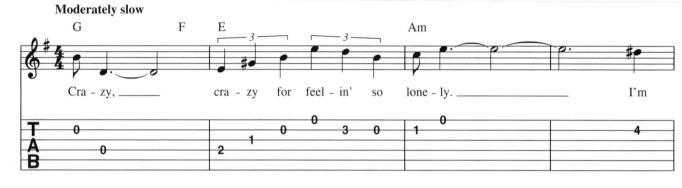

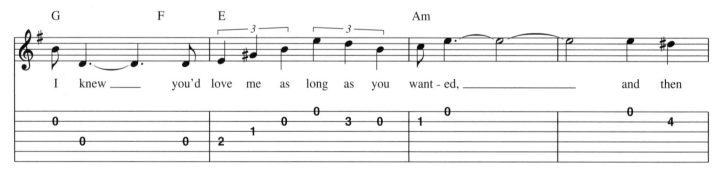

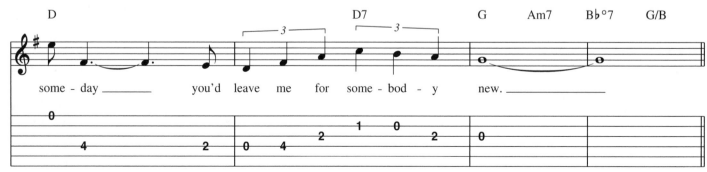

Bridge

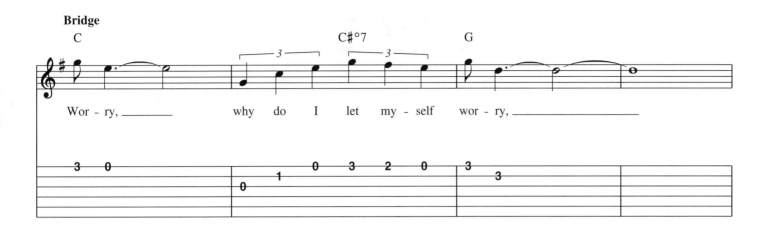

Wor - ry, _____ why do I let my - self wor - ry, _____

won - d'rin' _____ what in the world did I do? _____

Outro

Cra - zy _____ for think - ing that my love could hold you. _____ I'm

cra - zy for try - in', cra - zy for cry - in' and I'm cra - zy for lov - in' you.

Elvira

Words and Music by Dallas Frazier

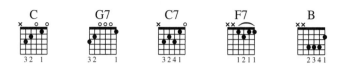

Strum Pattern: 4
Pick Pattern: 4

Intro

Moderate Country

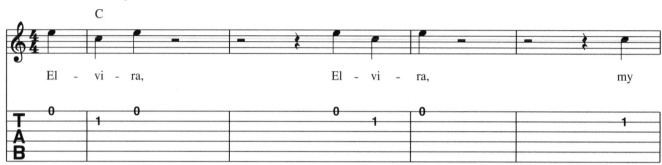

El - vi - ra,   El - vi - ra,   my

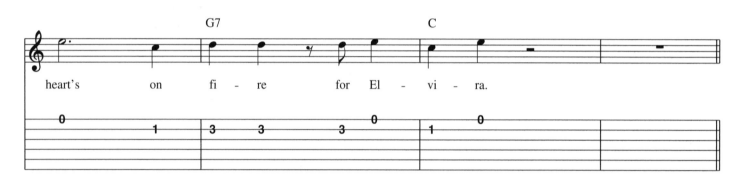

heart's   on   fi - re   for   El - vi - ra.

Verse

1. Eyes that look like heav - en.   Lips like cher - ry wine.   That girl can sho' nuff
2. *See additional lyrics*

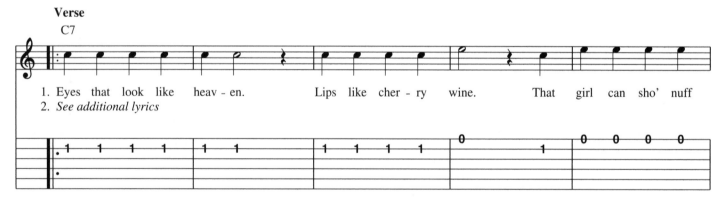

make my lit - tle light shine. _____   I get a fun - ny

Additional Lyrics

2. Tonight I'm gonna meet her at the Hungry House Cafe,
   And I'm gonna give her all the love I can.
   She's gonna jump and holler 'cause I saved up my last two dollars,
   And we're gonna search and find that preacher man.

Faded Love

Words and Music by Bob Wills and Johnny Wills

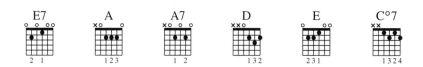

Strum Pattern: 1, 3
Pick Pattern: 2, 4

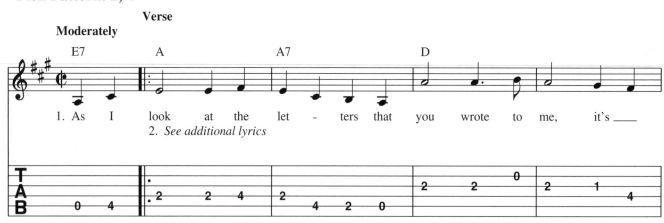

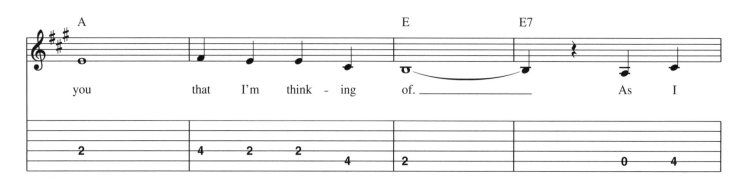

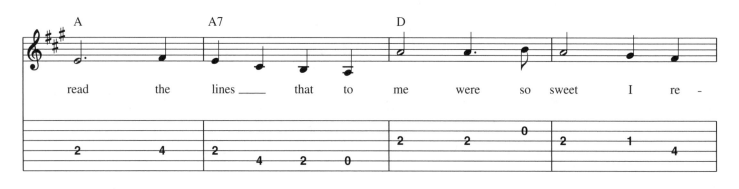

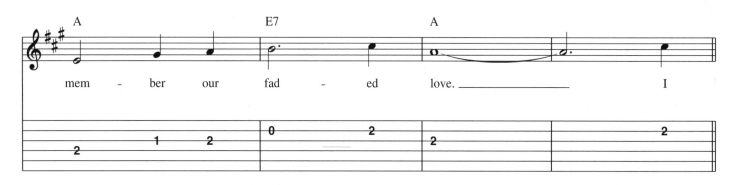

Chorus

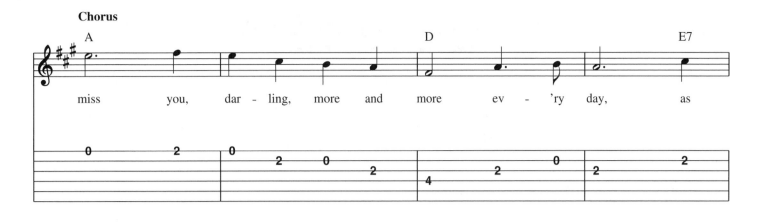

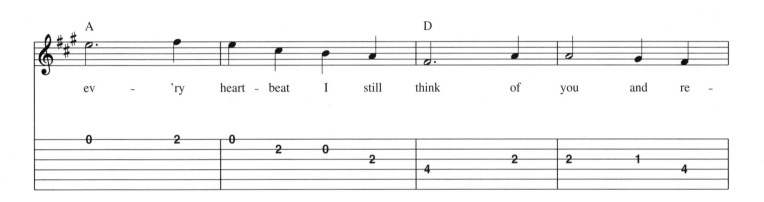

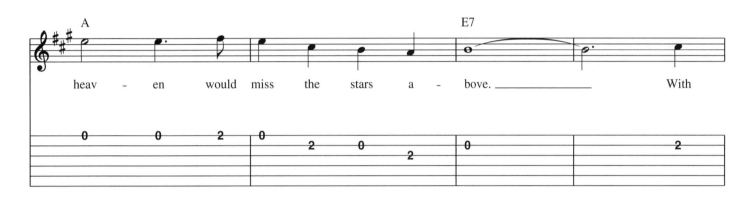

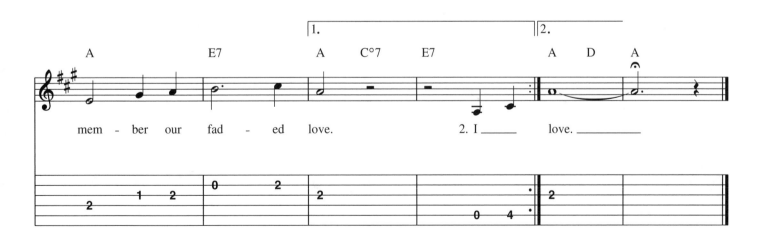

Additional Lyrics

2. I think of the past and all the pleasures we had
   As I watch the mating of the dove.
   It was the springtime that you said goodbye,
   I remember our faded love.

Folsom Prison Blues

Words and Music by John R. Cash

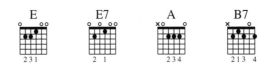

Strum Pattern: 3
Pick Pattern: 3

Intro

Moderately fast

1. I

Verse

hear the train a - com - in', it's roll - in' 'round the bend, and

2., 3., 4. *See additional lyrics*

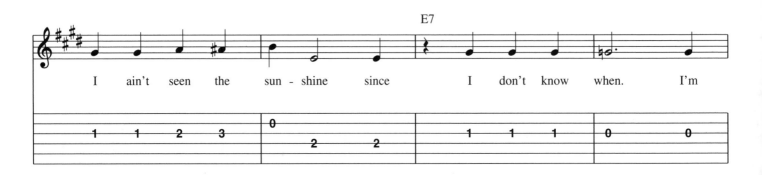

I ain't seen the sun - shine since I don't know when. I'm

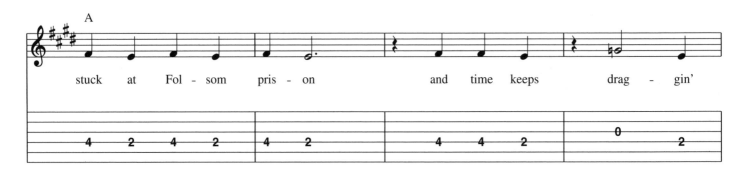

stuck at Fol - som pris - on and time keeps drag - gin'

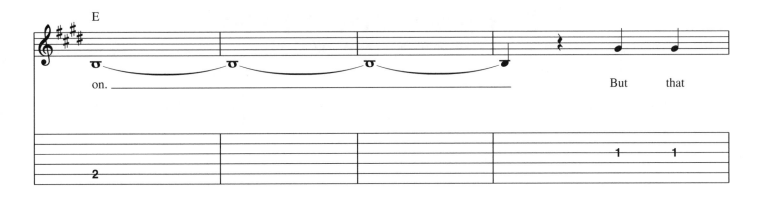

on. ___ But that

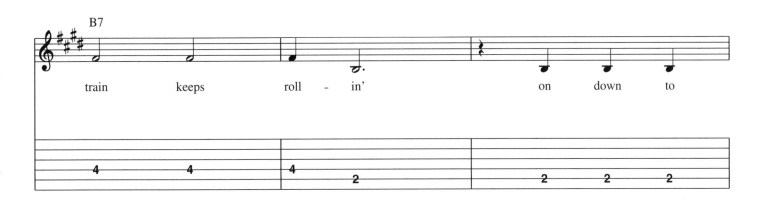

train keeps roll - in' on down to

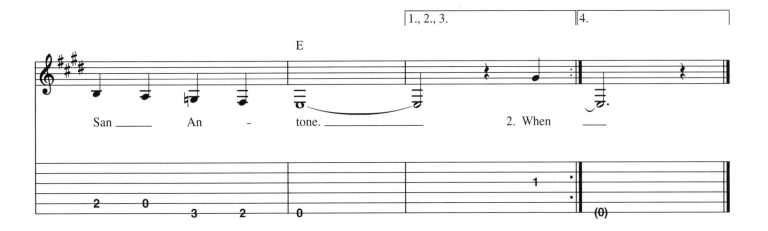

San ___ An - tone. ___ 2. When ___

Additional Lyrics

2. When I was just a baby my mama told me son,
   Always be a good boy; don't ever play with guns.
   But I shot a man in Reno, just to watch him die.
   When I hear that whistle blowin' I hang my head and cry.

3. I bet there's rich folks eatin' in a fancy dining car.
   They're prob'ly drinkin' coffee and smokin' big cigars,
   But I know I had it comin', I know I can't be free,
   But those people keep a-movin', and that's what tortures me.

4. Well, if they freed me from this prison, if that railroad train was mine,
   I bet I'd move on over a little farther down the line,
   Far from Folsom prison, that's where I want to stay.
   And I'd let that lonesome whistle blow my blues away.

For the Good Times

Words and Music by Kris Kristofferson

Chorus

Additional Lyrics

2. I'll get along; you'll find another;
   And I'll be here if you should find you ever need me.
   Don't say a word about tomorrow or forever.
   There'll be time enough for sadness when you leave me.

Forever and Ever, Amen

Words and Music by Paul Overstreet and Don Schlitz

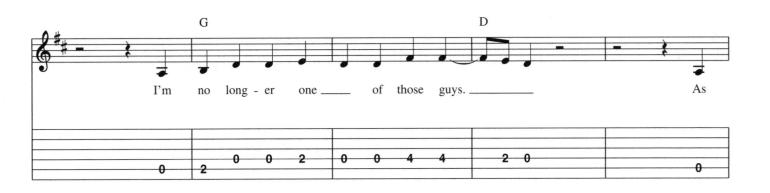

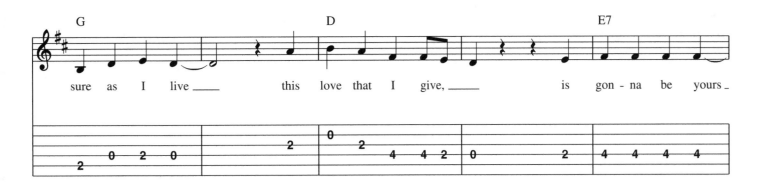

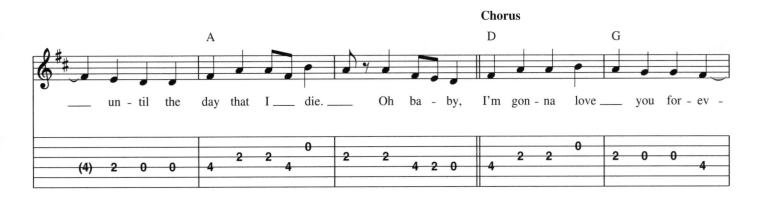

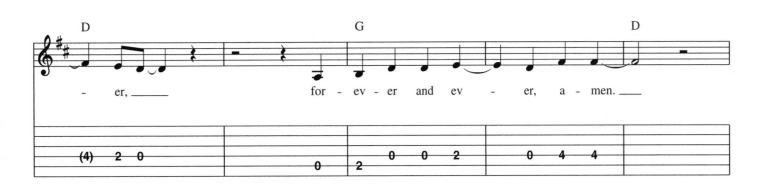

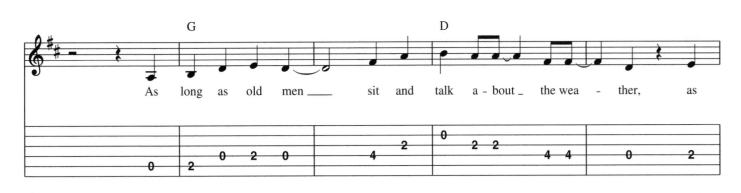

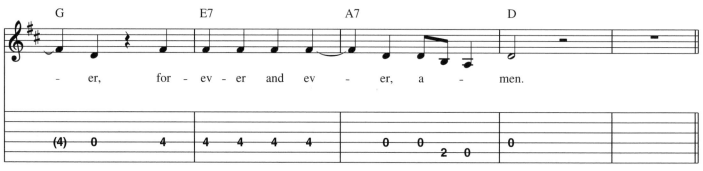

Interlude

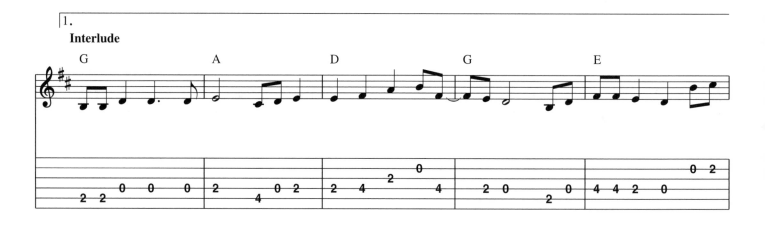

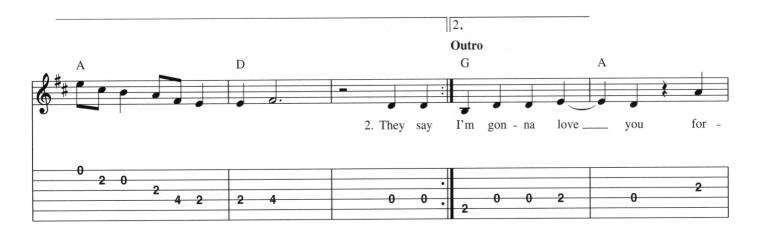

Outro

2. They say I'm gon-na love ___ you for -

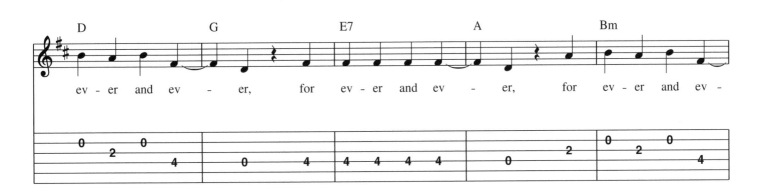

ev - er and ev - er, for ev - er and ev - er, for ev - er and ev -

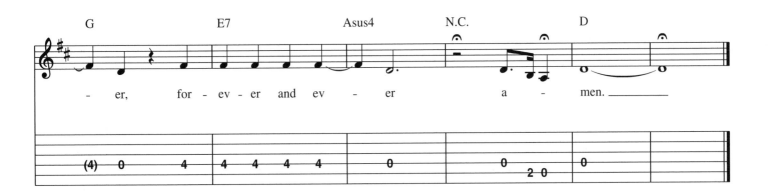

- er, for - ev - er and ev - er a - men. ___

Additional Lyrics

2. They say time takes its toll on a body,
Makes a young girl's brown hair turn gray.
Well, honey, I don't care,
I ain't in love with your hair,
And if it all fell out, well,
I'd love you anyway.
They say time can play tricks on a mem'ry.
Make people forget things they knew.
Well, it's easy to see it's happenin' to me.
I've already forgotten ev'ry woman but you. Oh darlin',...

Friends in Low Places

Words and Music by Dewayne Blackwell and Earl Bud Lee

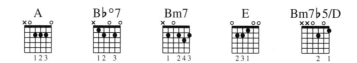

Strum Pattern: 4, 6
Pick Pattern: 1, 3

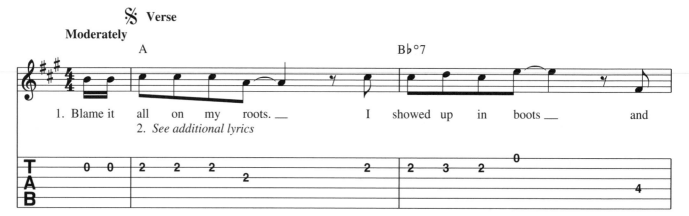

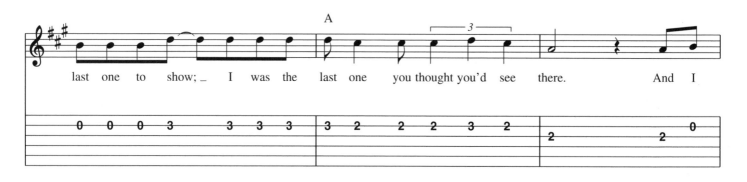

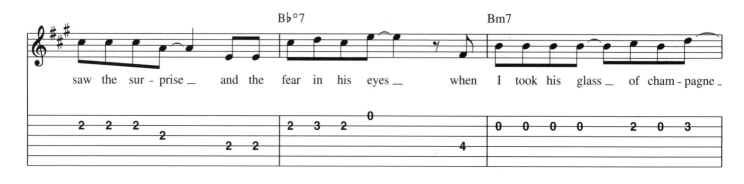

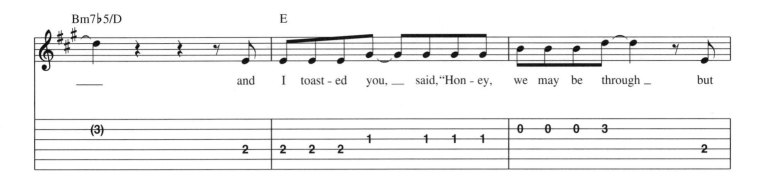

and I toast-ed you, ___ said, "Hon-ey, we may be through ___ but

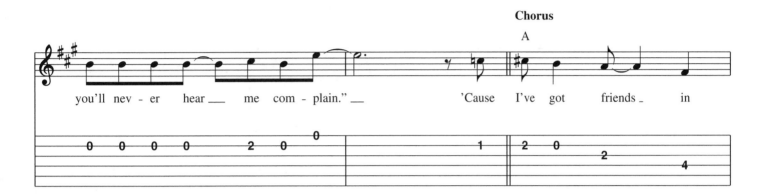

Chorus

you'll nev-er hear ___ me com-plain." ___ 'Cause I've got friends ___ in

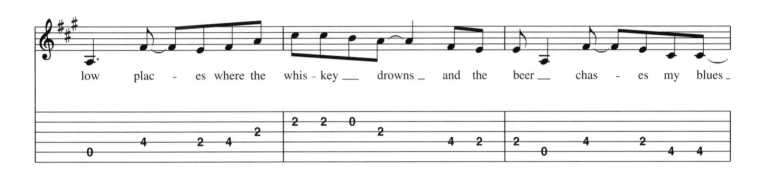

low plac - es where the whis-key ___ drowns ___ and the beer ___ chas - es my blues ___

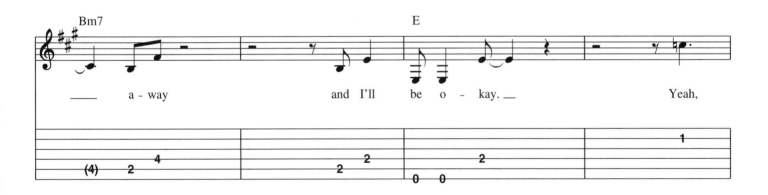

___ a-way and I'll be o - kay. ___ Yeah,

I'm not big ___ on so - cial grac - es. Think I'll slip on ___ down ___ to the

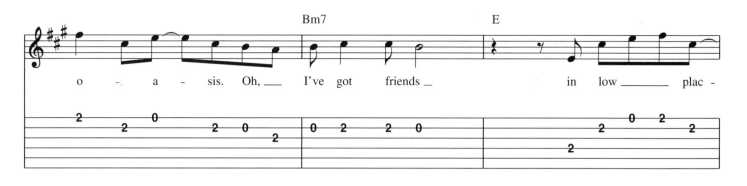

o - a - sis. Oh, ___ I've got friends ___ in low _____ plac -

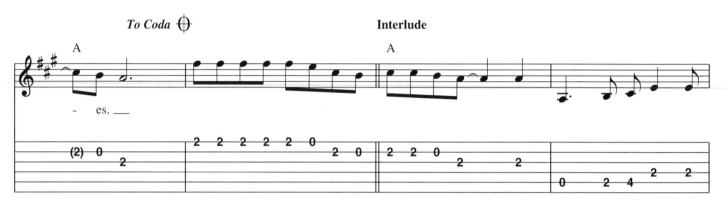

To Coda ⊕ **Interlude**

- es. ___

D.S. al Coda ⊕ **Coda**

2. Well, I

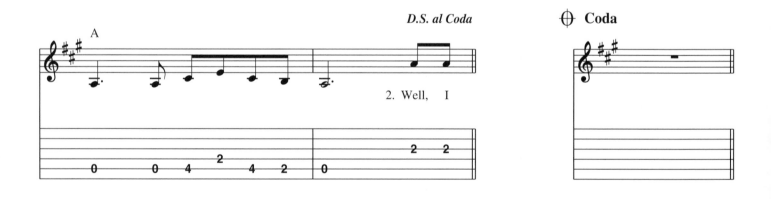

Outro-Chorus

I've got friends ___ in low plac - es where the whis - key ___ drowns ___ and the

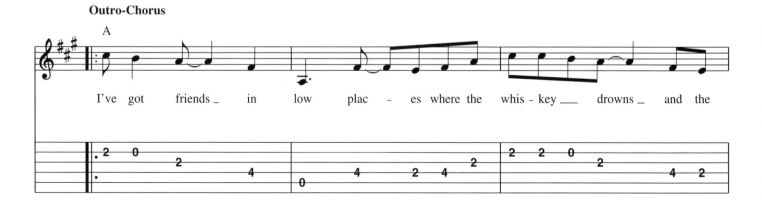

42

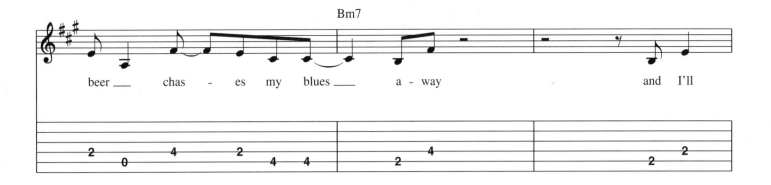

beer ___ chas - es my blues ___ a - way   and I'll

be o - kay. ___   Yeah, I'm not big ___ on

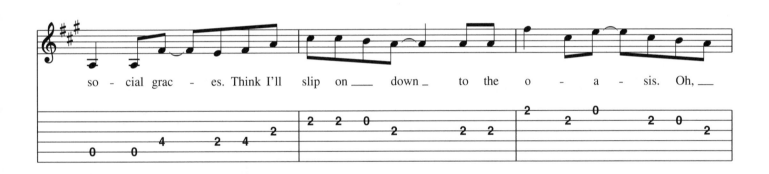

so - cial grac - es. Think I'll slip on ___ down _ to the o - a - sis. Oh, ___

Repeat and fade

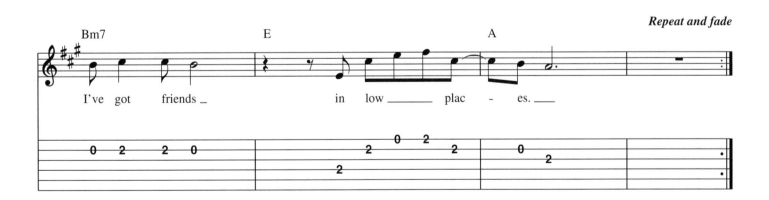

I've got friends _   in low _____ plac - es. ___

Additional Lyrics

2. Well, I guess I was wrong. I just don't belong,
   But then I've been there before.
   Ev'rything's alright. I'll just say goodnight
   And I'll show myself to the door.
   Hey, I didn't mean to cause a big scene
   Just give me an hour and then,
   Well, I'll be as high as that ivory tower
   That you're livin' in.

The Gambler

Words and Music by Don Schlitz

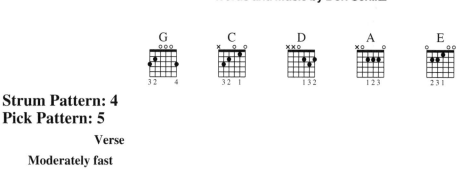

Strum Pattern: 4
Pick Pattern: 5

Verse

Moderately fast

1. On a warm sum-mer's eve - nin' on a train bound for no - where I
2. *See additional lyrics*

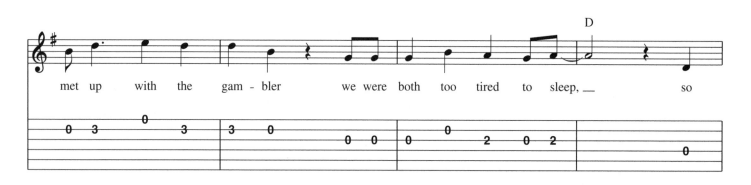

met up with the gam - bler we were both too tired to sleep, ___ so

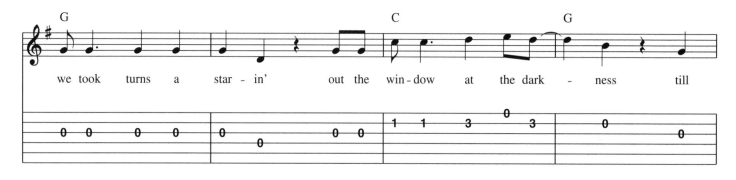

we took turns a star - in' out the win-dow at the dark - ness till

1.

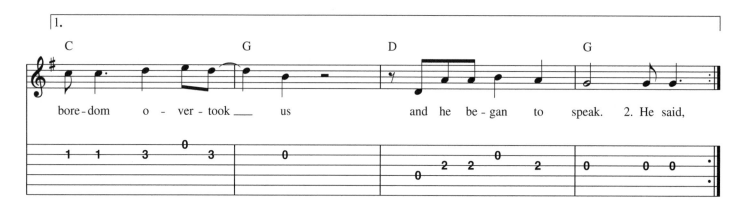

bore-dom o - ver-took ___ us and he be - gan to speak. 2. He said,

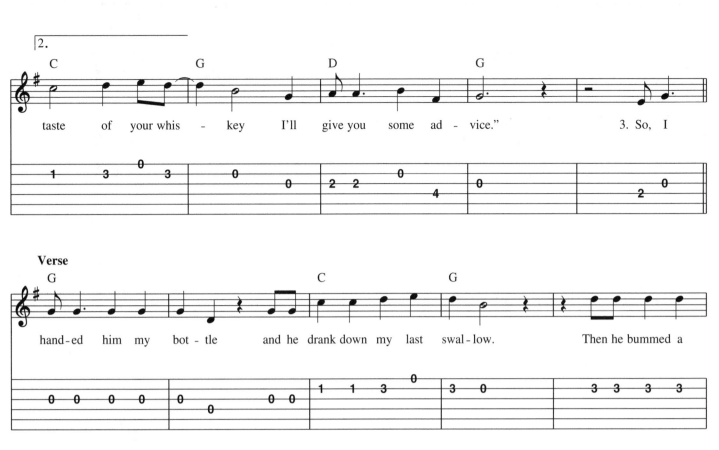

taste of your whis - key I'll give you some ad - vice." 3. So, I

Verse

hand - ed him my bot - tle and he drank down my last swal - low. Then he bummed a

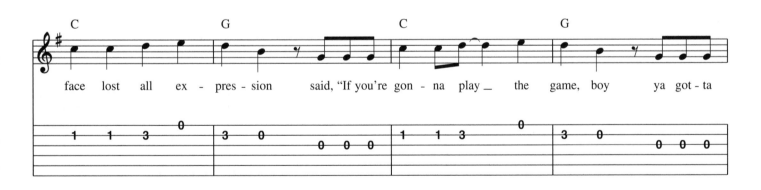

cig - a - rette _ and asked me for a light. _ And the night got death - ly qui - et, and his

face lost all ex - pres - sion said, "If you're gon - na play _ the game, boy ya got - ta

Chorus

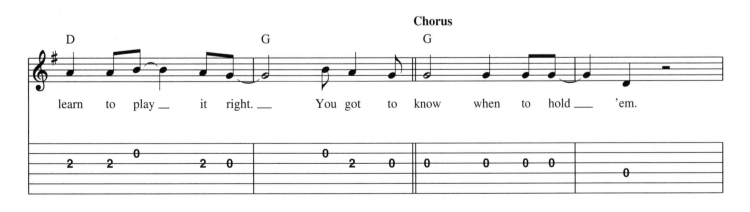

learn to play _ it right. _ You got to know when to hold _ 'em.

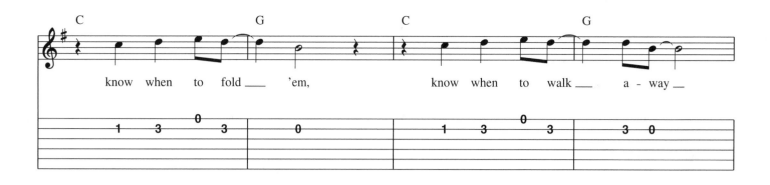

know when to fold ___ 'em,   know when to walk __ a - way __

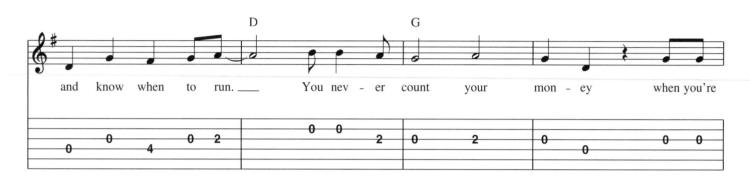

and know when to run. __ You nev - er count your mon - ey when you're

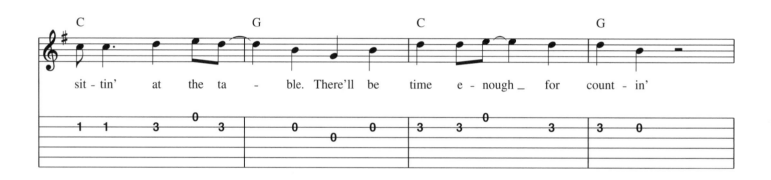

sit - tin' at the ta - ble. There'll be time e - nough _ for count - in'

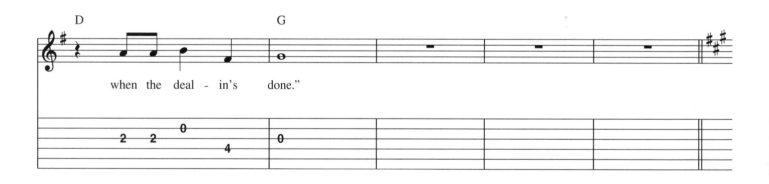

when the deal - in's done."

Verse

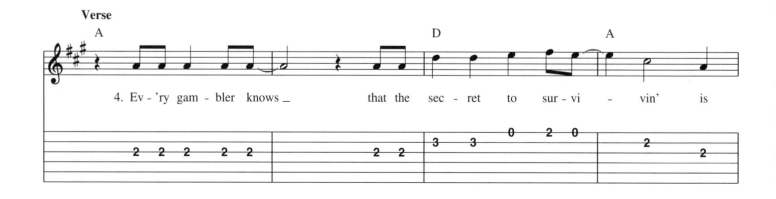

4. Ev - 'ry gam - bler knows _ that the sec - ret to sur - vi - vin' is

Additional Lyrics

2. He said, "Son I've made a life out of readin' people's faces,
   And knowing what their cards were by the way they held their eyes.
   And if you don't mind my sayin' I can see you're out of aces,
   For a taste of whiskey I'll give you some advice."

He'll Have to Go

Words and Music by Joe Allison and Audrey Allison

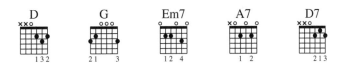

Strum Pattern: 7, 8
Pick Pattern: 7, 8

Verse
Moderately

1. Put your (2.) sweet lips a lit - tle clos - er to the phone. _____ Let's pre -

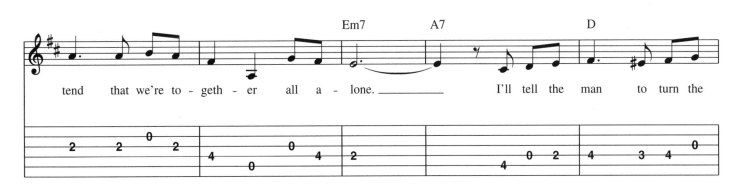

tend that we're to - geth - er all a - lone. _____ I'll tell the man to turn the

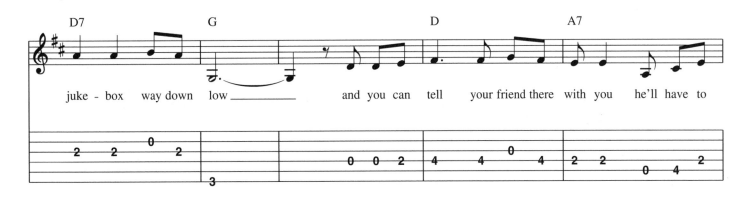

juke - box way down low _____ and you can tell your friend there with you he'll have to

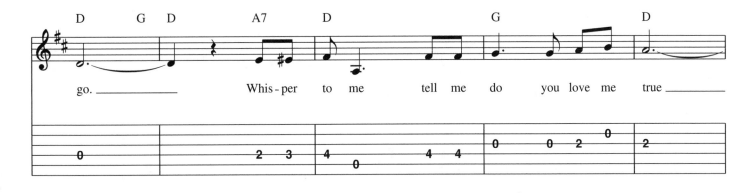

go. _____ Whis - per to me tell me do you love me true _____

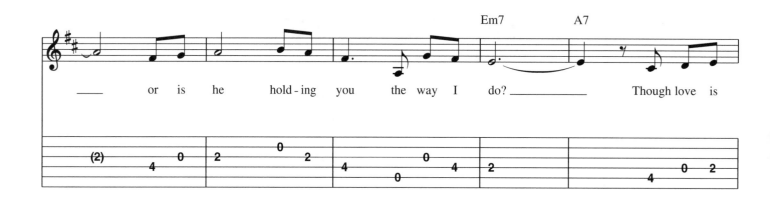

or is he hold-ing you the way I do? _____ Though love is

blind make up your mind I've got to know. _____ Should I hang up or will you

Bridge

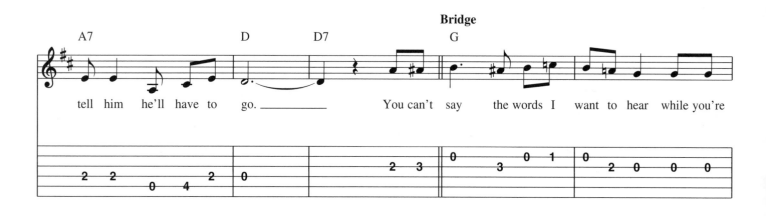

tell him he'll have to go. _____ You can't say the words I want to hear while you're

with an-oth-er man. If you want me, an-swer "Yes" or "No", dar-ling, I will un-der-

Outro

stand. Put your sweet lips a lit-tle clos-er to the phone. _____ Let's pre-

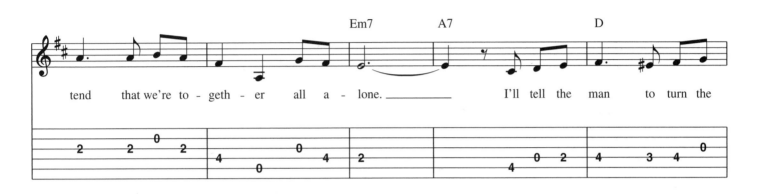

tend that we're to-geth-er all a-lone. _____ I'll tell the man to turn the

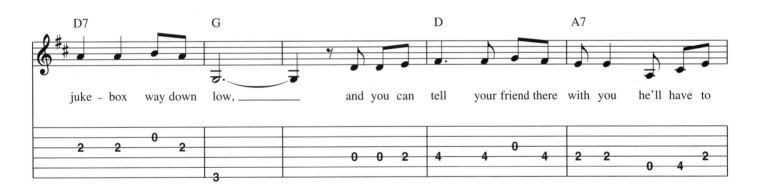

juke-box way down low, _____ and you can tell your friend there with you he'll have to

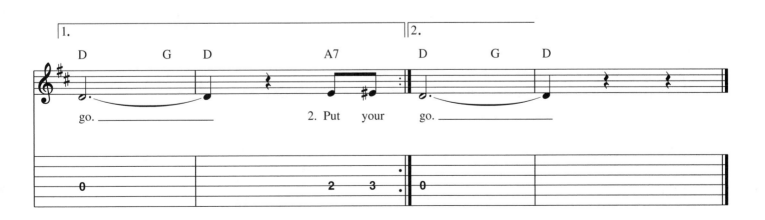

1.
go. _____ 2. Put your

2.
go. _____

Georgia on My Mind

Words by Stuart Gorrell
Music by Hoagy Carmichael

Bridge

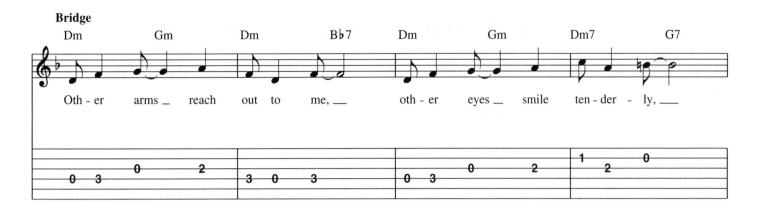

Oth - er arms ___ reach out to me, ___ oth - er eyes ___ smile ten - der - ly, ___

still in peace - ful dreams I see ___ the road leads back to you. _____

Outro

Geor - gia, _____ Geor - gia, _____ no peace I find, just an

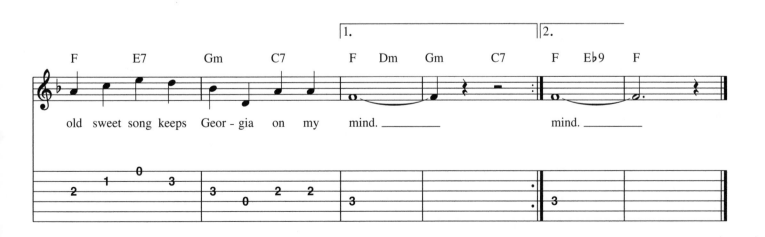

old sweet song keeps Geor - gia on my mind. _____ mind. _____

Green Green Grass of Home

Words and Music by Curly Putman

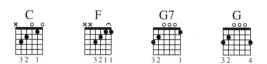

Strum Pattern: 6
Pick Pattern: 3

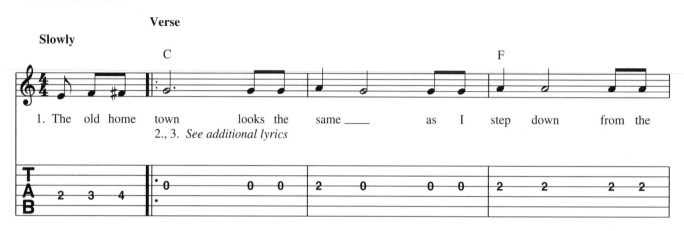

1. The old home town looks the same ____ as I step down from the
2., 3. *See additional lyrics*

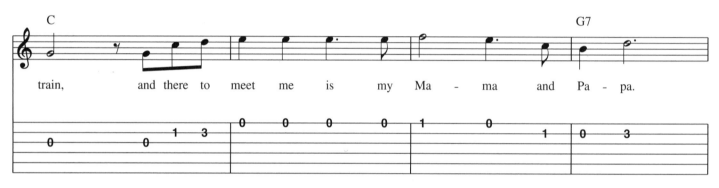

train, and there to meet me is my Ma - ma and Pa - pa.

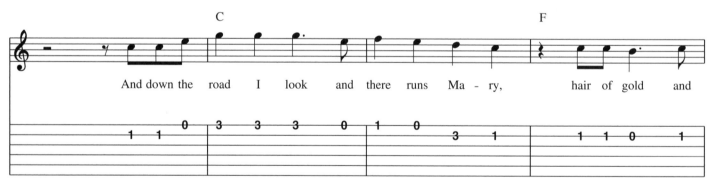

And down the road I look and there runs Ma - ry, hair of gold and

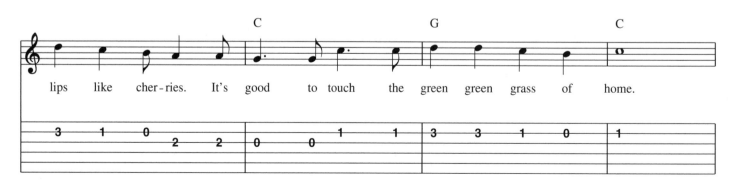

lips like cher - ries. It's good to touch the green green grass of home.

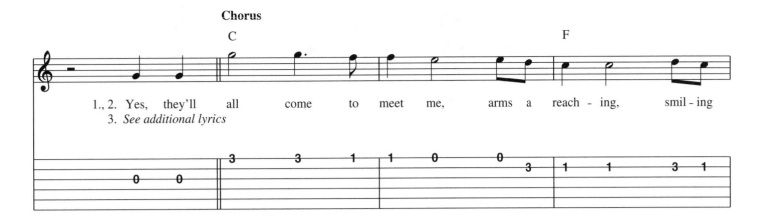

Chorus

1., 2. Yes, they'll all come to meet me, arms a reach - ing, smil - ing
3. *See additional lyrics*

sweet - ly. It's good to touch the green green grass of

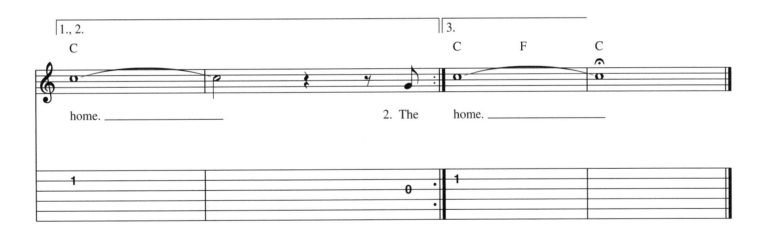

home. 2. The home.

Additional Lyrics

2. The old house is still standing though the paint is cracked and dry,
   And there's that old oak tree that I used to play on.
   Down the lane I walk with my sweet Mary, hair of gold and lips like cherries.
   It's good to touch the green green grass of home.

3. *Spoken:* *Then I awake and look around me at the gray walls that surround me,*
   And I realize that I was only dreaming.
   For there's a guard and there's a sad old Padre, arm in arm we'll walk at daybreak,
   Again I'll touch the green green grass of home.

Chorus 3. Yes, they'll all come to see me in the shade of that old oak tree,
   As they lay me 'neath the green green grass of home.

He Stopped Loving Her Today

Words and Music by Bobby Braddock and Curly Putman

Strum Pattern: 4
Pick Pattern: 3

hop - ing she'd come back a - gain. First time I'd seen him smile in years. _____

Chorus

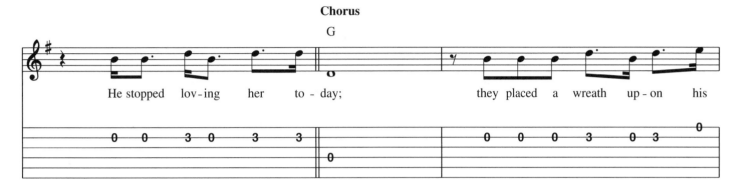

He stopped lov - ing her to - day; they placed a wreath up - on his

door, _____ and soon they'll car - ry him a - way; _____

To Coda ⊕   ***D.S. al Coda***
(take 2nd ending)   ⊕ **Coda**

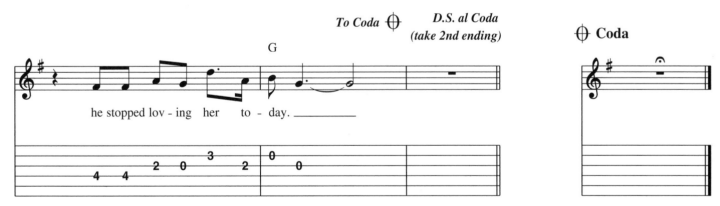

he stopped lov - ing her to - day. _____

Additional Lyrics

3. He kept some letters by his bed,
   Dated nineteen-sixty-two;
   He had underlined in red
   Ev'ry single "I love you."

4. I went to see him just today,
   But I didn't see no tears.
   All dressed up to go away;
   First time I'd seen him smile in years.

5. *Spoken: She came to see him one last time;*
   We all wondered if she would,
   And it kept running through my mind,
   This time he's over her for good.

Help Me Make It Through the Night

Words and Music by Kris Kristofferson

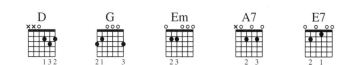

Strum Pattern: 1, 4
Pick Pattern: 1, 3

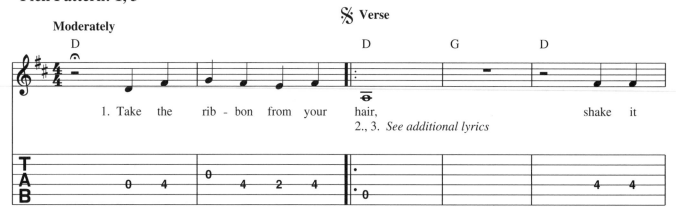

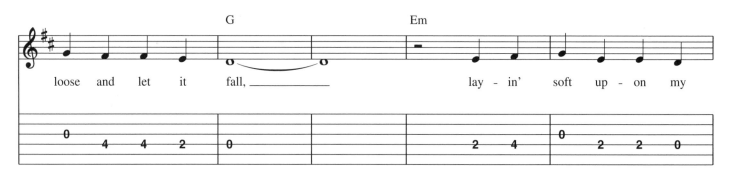

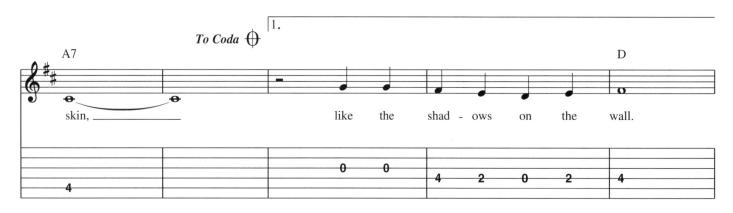

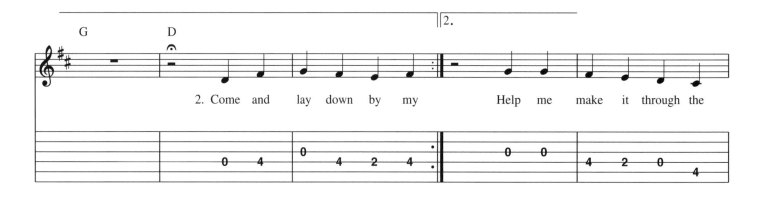

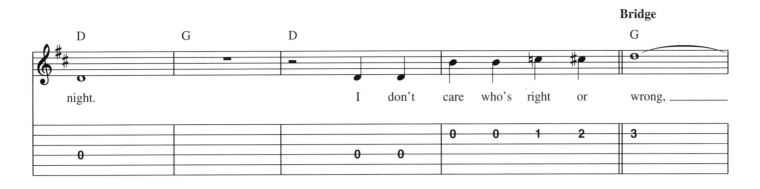

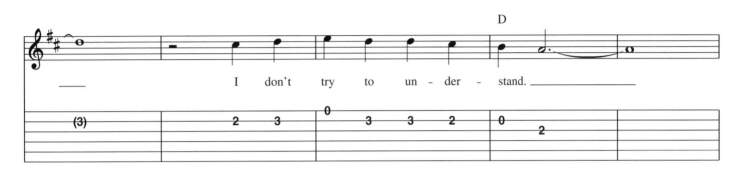

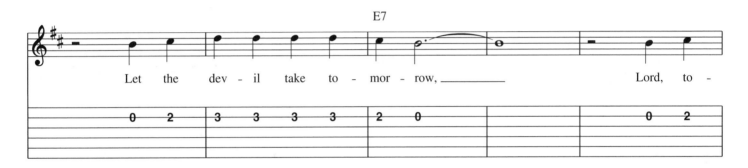

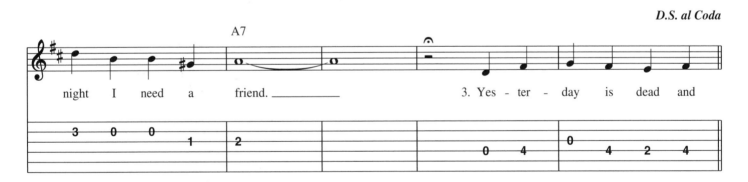

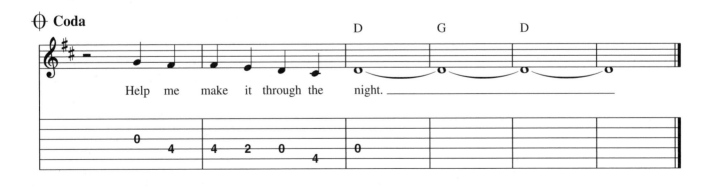

Additional Lyrics

2. Come and lay down by my side
Till the early mornin' light.
All I'm takin' is your time.
Help me make it through the night.

3. Yesterday is dead and gone
And tomorrow's out of sight,
And it's sad to be alone.
Help me make it through the night.

Hey, Good Lookin'

Words and Music by Hank Williams

Additional Lyrics

2. I'm free and ready so we can go steady.
How's about savin' all your time for me?
No more lookin', I know I've been tooken.
How's about keepin' steady company?

Bridge I'm gonna throw my date book over the fence
And find me one for five or ten cents.
I'll keep it till it's covered with age,
'Cause I'm writin' your name down on ev'ry page.

I Can't Stop Loving You

Words and Music by Don Gibson

Additional Lyrics

Chorus I can't stop loving you, there's no use to try.
Pretend there's someone new; I can't live a lie.
I can't stop wanting you the way that I do.
There's only been one love for me, that one love is you.

I Fall to Pieces

Words and Music by Hank Cochran and Harlan Howard

Strum Pattern: 3
Pick Pattern: 3

Chorus

Moderately

See additional lyrics

I fall _____ to piec - es, _____

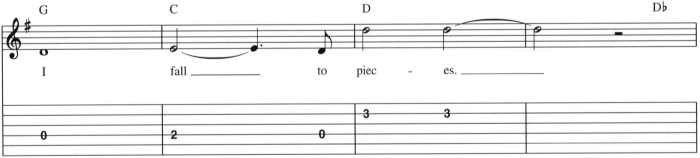

each time I see you a - gain.

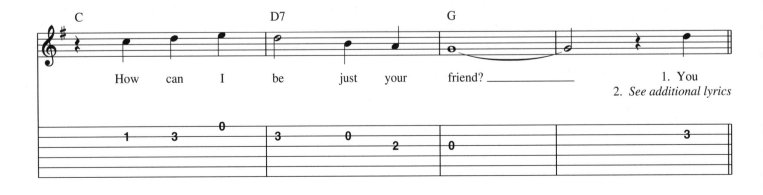

I fall _____ to piec - es. _____

How can I be just your friend? _____

1. You
2. *See additional lyrics*

Additional Lyrics

Chorus I fall to pieces each time someone speaks your name.
I fall to pieces. Time only adds to the flame.

2. You tell me to find someone else to love,
Someone who'll love me too, the way you used to do.
But each time I go out with someone new,
You walk by and I fall to pieces.

I Walk the Line

Words and Music by John R. Cash

Strum Pattern: 1, 3
Pick Pattern: 3, 4

Verse

Moderately bright

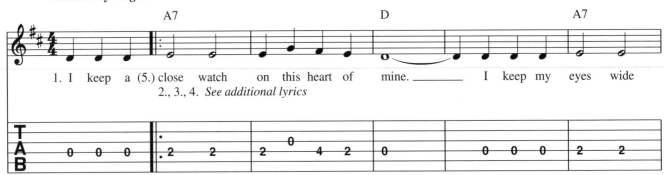

1. I keep a (5.) close watch on this heart of mine. _____ I keep my eyes wide
2., 3., 4. *See additional lyrics*

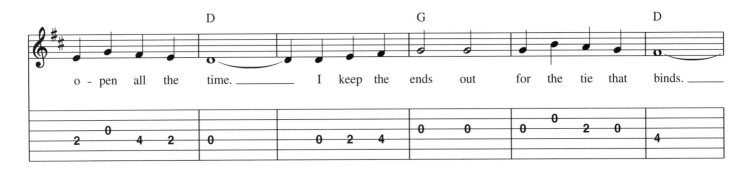

o - pen all the time. _____ I keep the ends out for the tie that binds. _____

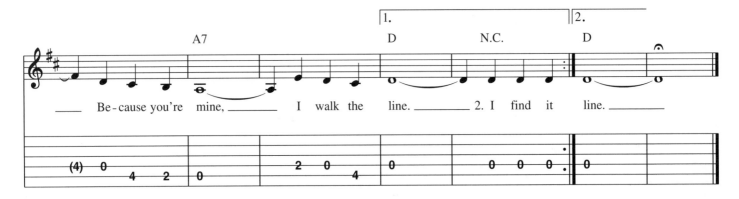

_____ Be - cause you're mine, _____ I walk the line. _____ 2. I find it line. _____

Additional Lyrics

2. I find it very, very easy to be true.
   I find myself alone when each day is through.
   Yes, I'll admit that I'm a fool for you.
   Because you're mine, I walk the line.

3. As sure as night is dark and day is light,
   I keep you on my mind both day and night.
   And happiness I've known proves that it's right.
   Because you're mine, I walk the line.

4. You've got a way to keep me on your side.
   You give me cause for love that I can't hide.
   For you I know I'd even try to turn the tide.
   Because you're mine, I walk the line.

Lookin' for Love

from URBAN COWBOY

Words and Music by Wanda Mallette, Patti Ryan and Bob Morrison

Additional Lyrics

2. And I was alone then, no love in sight;
   And I did ev'rything I could to get me through the night.
   Don't know where it started or where it might end;
   I turned to a stranger just like a friend.

I'm So Lonesome I Could Cry

Words and Music by Hank Williams

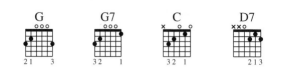

Strum Pattern: 7, 8
Pick Pattern: 7, 8

Verse

Moderately

1. Hear _____ that lone - some whip - poor - will, he
2. *See additional lyrics*

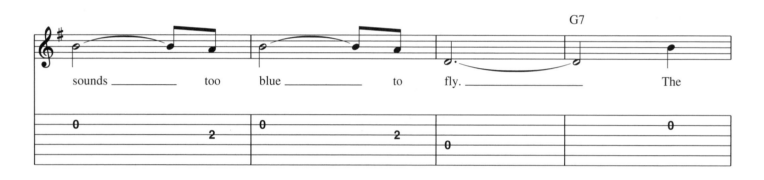

sounds _____ too blue _____ to fly. _____ The

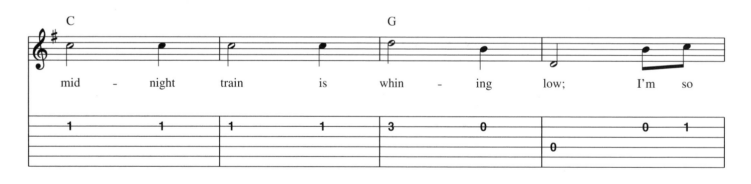

mid - night train is whin - ing low; I'm so

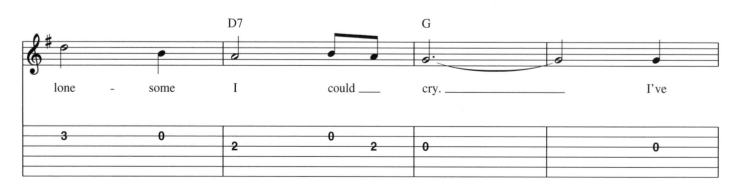

lone - some I could _____ cry. _____ I've

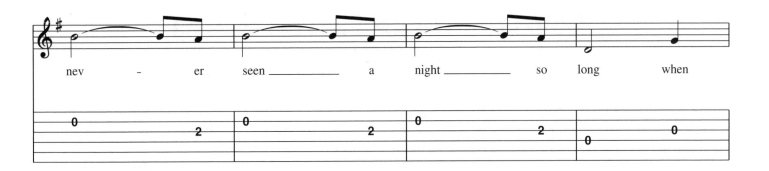

nev - er seen _____ a night _____ so long when

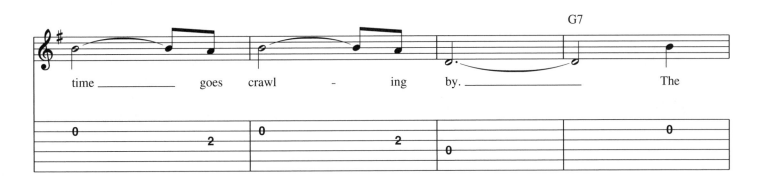

time _____ goes crawl - ing by. _____ The

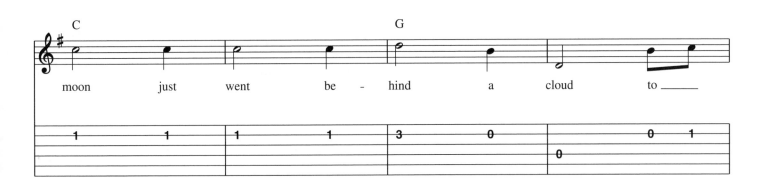

moon just went be - hind a cloud to _____

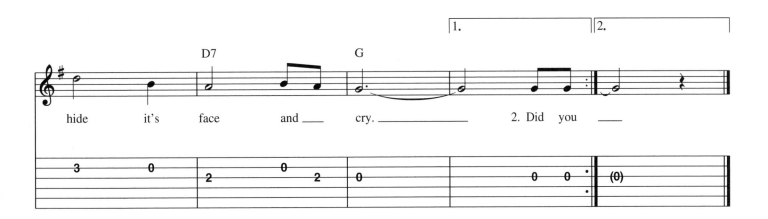

hide it's face and _____ cry. _____ 2. Did you _____

Additional Lyrics

2. Did you ever see a robin weep,
   When leaves began to die?
   That means he's lost the will to live.
   I'm so lonesome I could cry.
   The silence of a falling star
   Lights up a purple sky.
   And as I wonder where you are
   I'm so lonesome I could cry.

It Was Almost Like a Song

Lyric by Hal David
Music by Archie Jordan

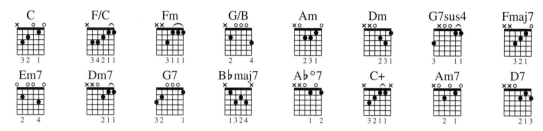

Strum Pattern: 2, 6
Pick Pattern: 5, 4

Verse

Moderately slow

Chorus

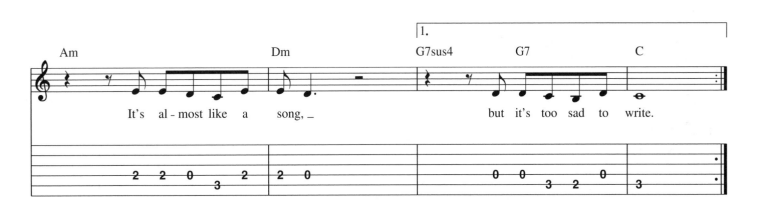

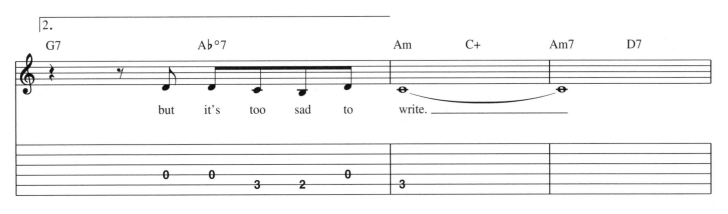

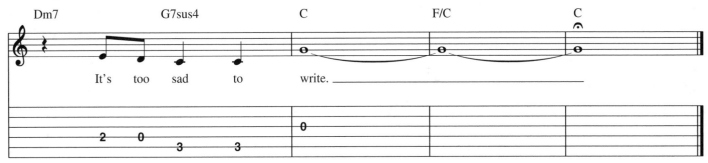

Additional Lyrics

2. You were in my arms.
Just where you belong.
We were so in love.
It was almost like a song.

Jambalaya
(On the Bayou)

Words and Music by Hank Williams

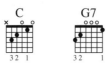

Strum Pattern: 2, 5
Pick Pattern: 3, 6

Verse

Moderately

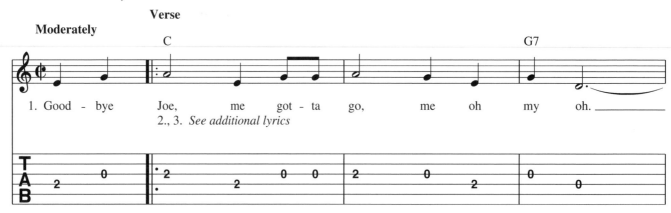

1. Good-bye Joe, me got-ta go, me oh my oh. _____
2., 3. *See additional lyrics*

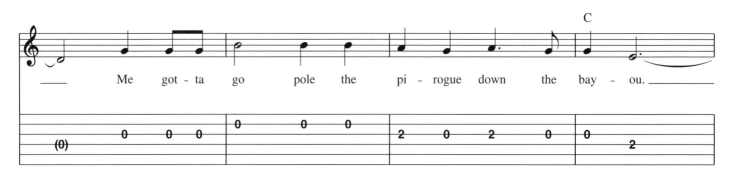

_____ Me got-ta go pole the pi - rogue down the bay - ou. _____

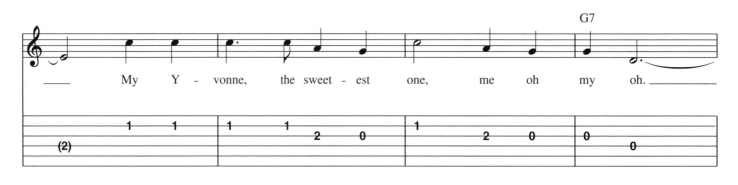

_____ My Y - vonne, the sweet - est one, me oh my oh. _____

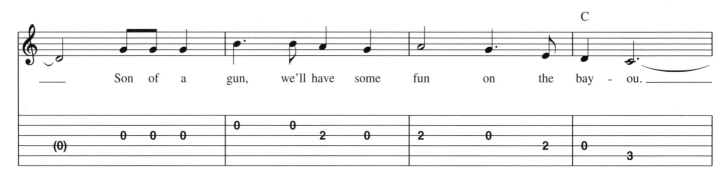

_____ Son of a gun, we'll have some fun on the bay - ou. _____

Additional Lyrics

2. Thi bo daux, Fontaineaux, the place is buzzin'.
   Kinfolk come to see Yvonne by the dozen.
   Dress in style and go hog wild, me oh, my oh.

3. Settle down far from town, get me a pirogue.
   And I'll catch all the fish in the bayou.
   Swap my mon to but Yvonne what we need-o.

King of the Road

Words and Music by Roger Miller

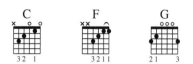

Strum Pattern: 3, 4
Pick Pattern: 1, 3

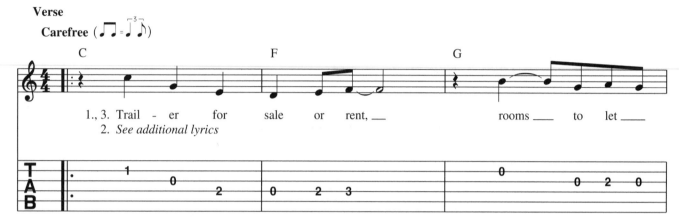

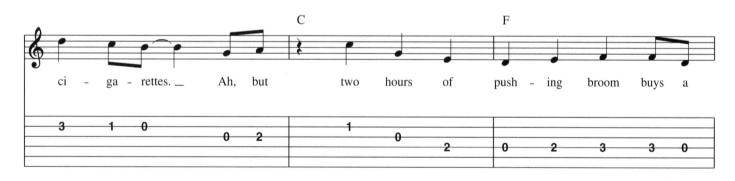

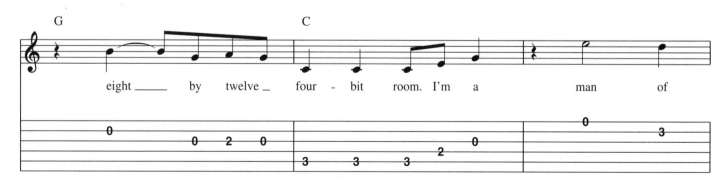

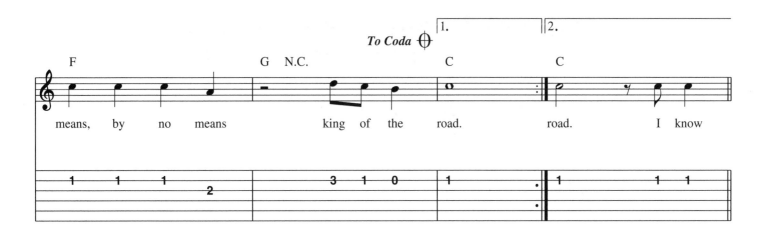

To Coda ⊕

means, by no means   king of the road.   road.   I know

Bridge

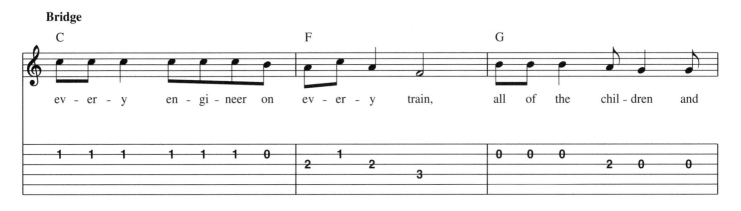

ev - er - y   en - gi - neer on   ev - er - y   train,   all of the   chil - dren   and

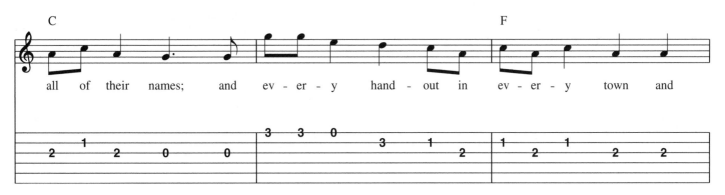

all of their names;   and ev - er - y   hand - out in   ev - er - y   town   and

D.C. al Coda   ⊕ **Coda**

ev - 'ry lock that ain't locked when   no one's a - round. I sing: road.

Additional Lyrics

2. Third boxcar, midnight train,
   Destination Bangor, Maine;
   Old worn out suit and shoes,
   I don't pay no union dues.
   I smoke old stogies I have found,
   Short but not too big around.
   I'm a man of means,
   By no means king of the road.

77

Kiss an Angel Good Mornin'

Words and Music by Ben Peters

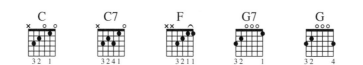

Strum Pattern: 6
Pick Pattern: 3

Verse
Moderately

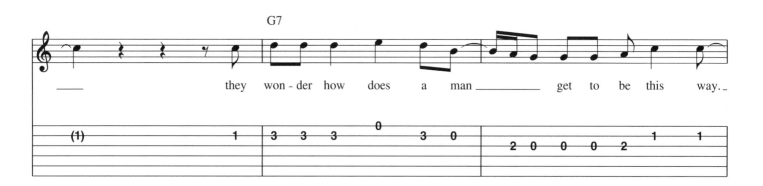

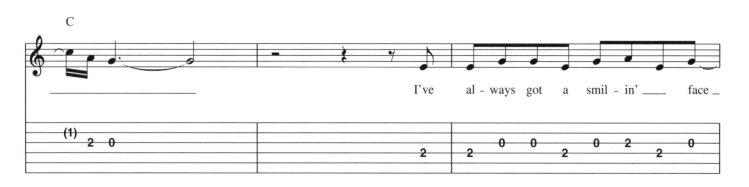

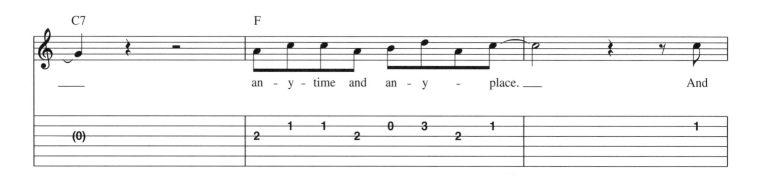

Additional Lyrics

2. Well, people may try to guess the secret of happiness,
   But some of them never learn it's a simple thing.
   The secret I'm speakin' of is a woman and a man in love,
   And the answer is in this song that I always sing.

Lucille

Words and Music by Roger Bowling and Hal Bynum

Strum Pattern: 7, 8
Pick Pattern: 7, 8

Verse

1. In a bar in _____ To - le - do a - cross from _____ the
2. *See additional lyrics*

de - pot, _____ on a bar stool _____ she took off her ring. _____ I

thought I'd get clos - er, so I walked _ on ___ o - ver, I sat down ___ and

asked her her name. _____ When the drinks fin - 'ly hit _____ her, she

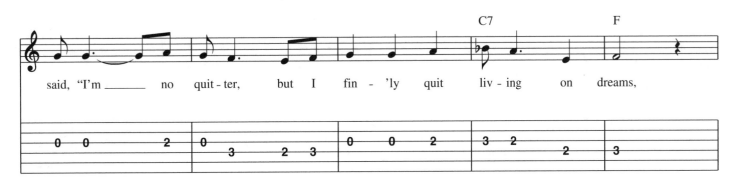

said, "I'm _____ no quit-ter, but I fin - 'ly quit liv - ing on dreams,

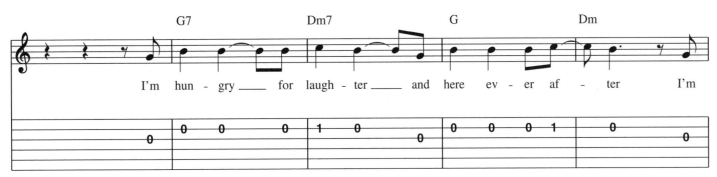

I'm hun - gry _____ for laugh - ter _____ and here ev - er af - ter I'm

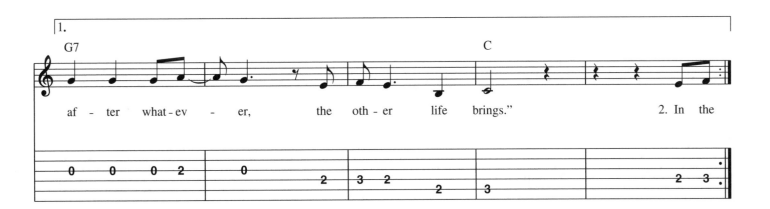

1.

af - ter what-ev - er, the oth - er life brings." 2. In the

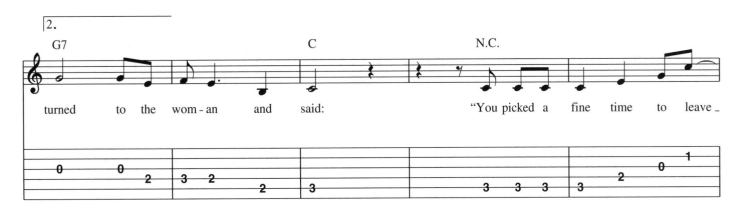

2.

turned to the wom-an and said: "You picked a fine time to leave _____

Chorus

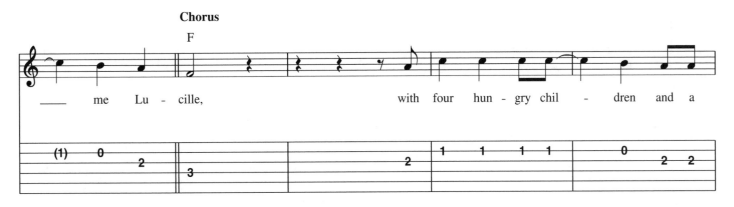

_____ me Lu - cille, with four hun - gry chil - dren and a

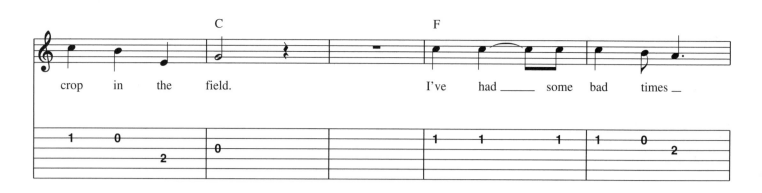

crop in the field.   I've had _____ some bad times _

lived through _ some sad times _ but this time _____ the hurt - in' won't heal.

You picked a fine time _____ to leave me Lu - cille."

Verse

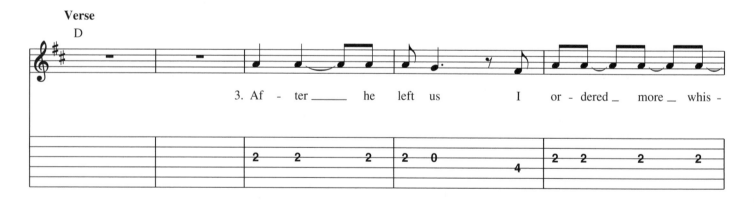

3. Af - ter _____ he left us   I or - dered _ more _ whis -

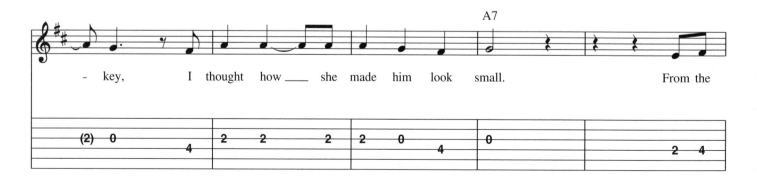

- key,   I thought how ____ she made him look small.   From the

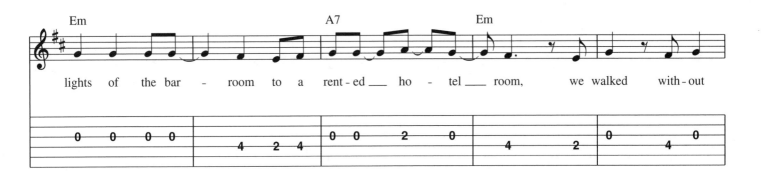

lights of the bar - room to a rent-ed ___ ho - tel ___ room, we walked with-out

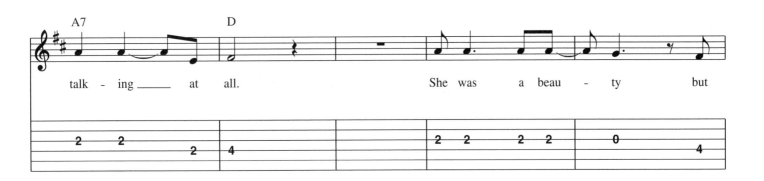

talk - ing ___ at all. She was a beau - ty but

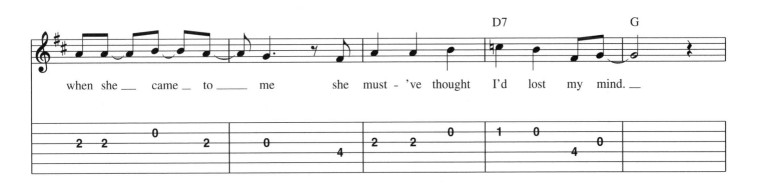

when she ___ came ___ to ___ me she must - 've thought I'd lost my mind. ___

I could - n't hold ___ her 'cause the words that he told ___ her kept

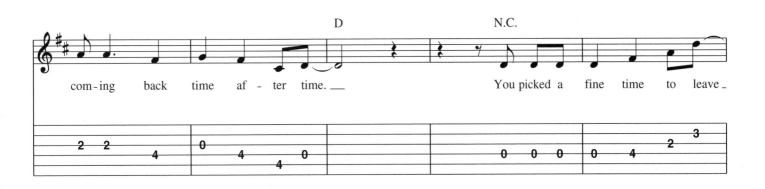

com-ing back time af - ter time. ___ You picked a fine time to leave ___

Chorus

me Lu - cille, with four hun - gry chil - dren and a

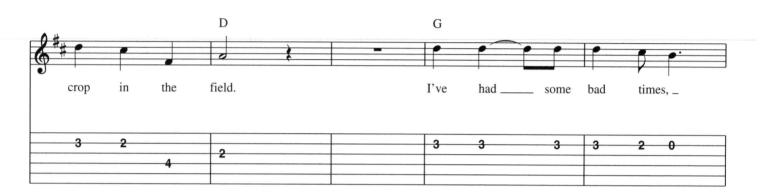

crop in the field. I've had ___ some bad times, _

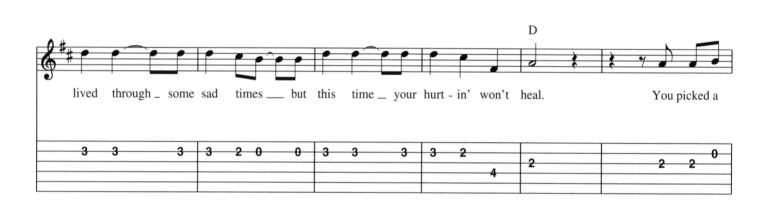

lived through _ some sad times _ but this time _ your hurt - in' won't heal. You picked a

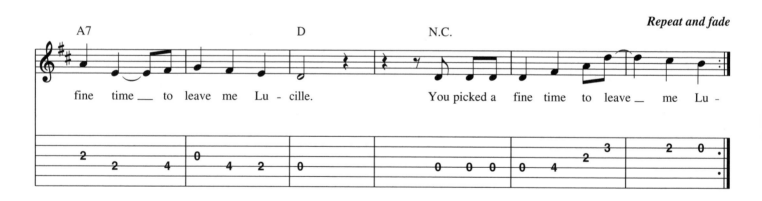

Repeat and fade

fine time _ to leave me Lu - cille. You picked a fine time to leave _ me Lu -

Additional Lyrics

2. In the mirror I saw him and I closely watched him,
   I thought how he looked out of place.
   He came to the woman who sat there beside me,
   He had a strange look on his face.
   The big hands were calloused, he looked like a mountain,
   For a minute I thought I was dead.
   But he started shaking, his big heart was breaking,
   He turned to the woman and said:

Make the World Go Away

Words and Music by Hank Cochran

Strum Pattern: 3, 4
Pick Pattern: 1, 3

Additional Lyrics

2. I'm sorry if I hurt you,
   I'll make it up day by day.
   Just say you love me like you used to,
   And make the world go away.

Night Life

Words and Music by Willie Nelson, Walt Breeland and Paul Buskirk

Strum Pattern: 3, 4
Pick Pattern: 1, 3

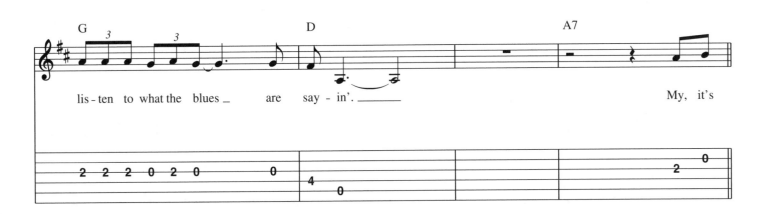

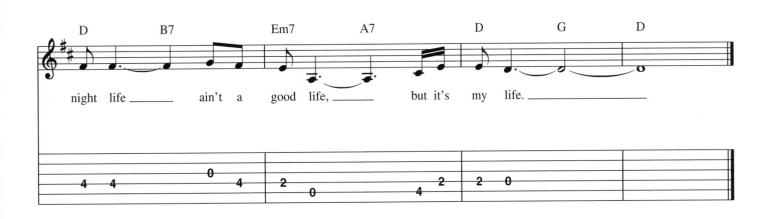

Oh, Lonesome Me

Words and Music by Don Gibson

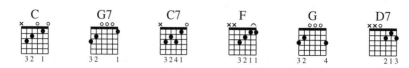

Strum Pattern: 4
Pick Pattern: 1

Chorus

Moderately

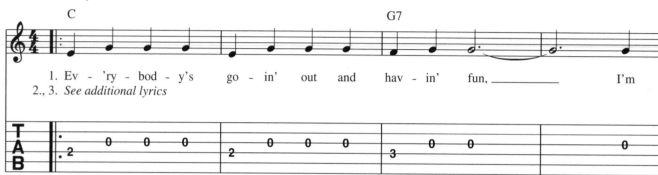

1. Ev - 'ry - bod - y's go - in' out and hav - in' fun, _____ I'm
2., 3. *See additional lyrics*

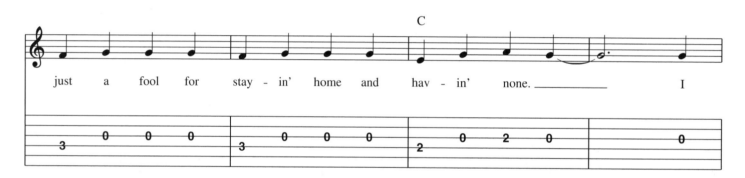

just a fool for stay - in' home and hav - in' none. _____ I

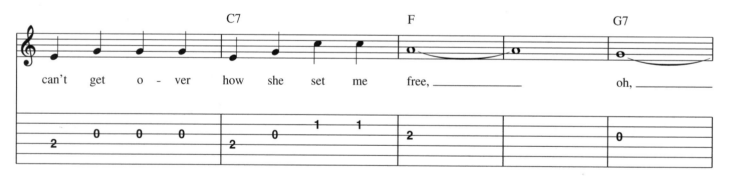

can't get o - ver how she set me free, _____ oh, _____

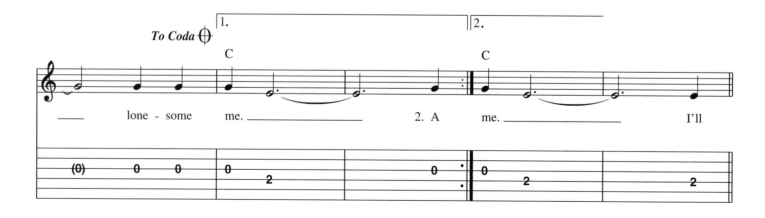

To Coda ⊕ |1. C | |2. C
_____ lone - some me. _____ 2. A me. _____ I'll

Bridge

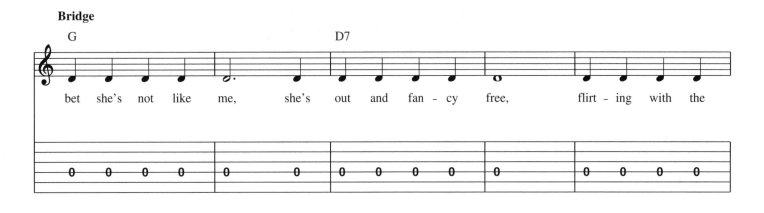

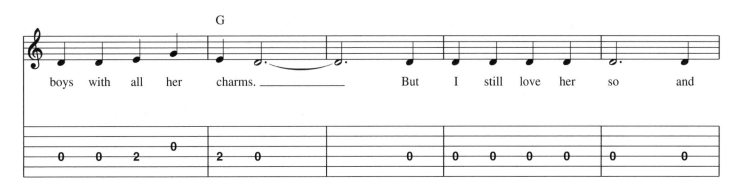

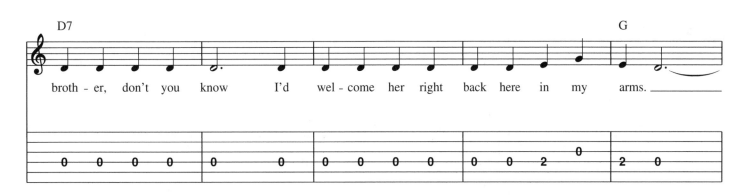

D.S. al Coda   ⊕ **Coda**

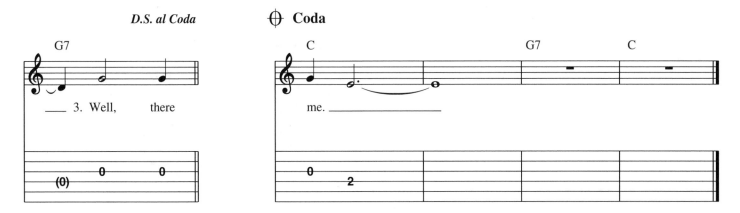

Additional Lyrics

2. A bad mistake I'm makin' just hangin' 'round,
   I know that I should have some fun and paint the town.
   A lovesick fool that's blind and just can't see,
   Oh, lonesome me.

3. Well, there must be some way I can lose these lonesome blues,
   Forget about the past and find somebody new.
   I've thought of everything from A to Z,
   Oh, lonesome me.

Okie From Muskogee

Words and Music by Merle Haggard and Roy Edward Burris

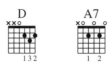

Strum Pattern: 2, 4
Pick Pattern: 1, 3

Verse

Moderately fast

we don't take our trips on L. S. D. And

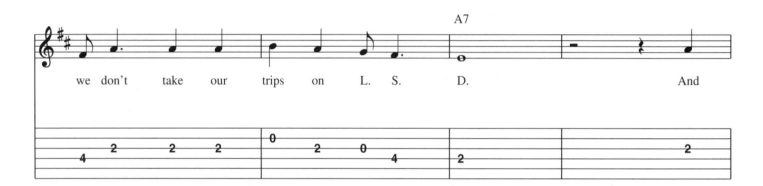

we don't burn our draft cards down on Main Street, but

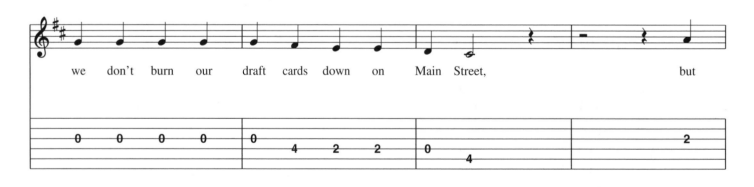

we like liv-ing right and be-ing free. _____ And I'm

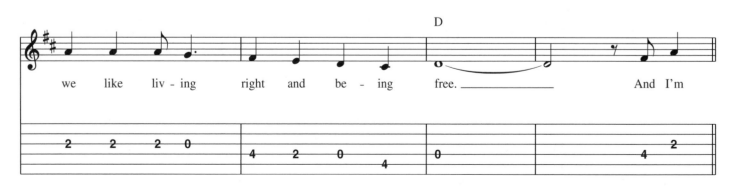

Chorus

proud   to   be   an   o - kie   from   Mus - ko - gee;   A

place   where   e - ven   squares   can   have   a   ball. ____

We   still   wave   Ol'   Glo - ry   down   at   the   Court   House,   white

light - ning's   still   the   big - gest   thrill   of   all. ____

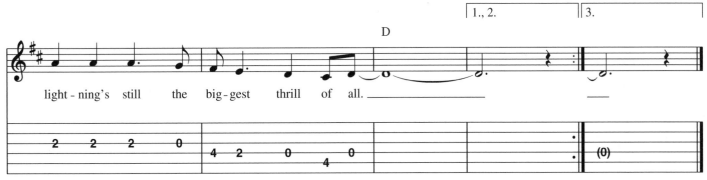

Additional Lyrics

2. We don't make a party out of loving,
   But we like holding hands and pitching woo.
   We don't let our hair grow long and shaggy,
   Like the hippies out in San Francisco do.

3. Leather boots are still in style if a man needs footwear.
   Beads and Roman sandals won't be seen.
   Football's still the roughest thing on campus,
   And the kids here still respect the college Dean.

Paper Roses

Words by Janice Torre
Music by Fred Spielman

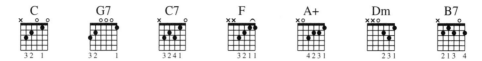

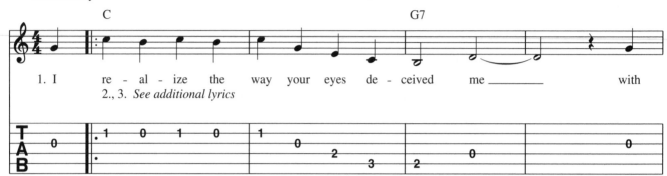

Strum Pattern: 4
Pick Pattern: 5

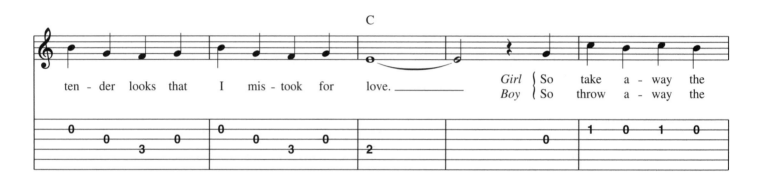

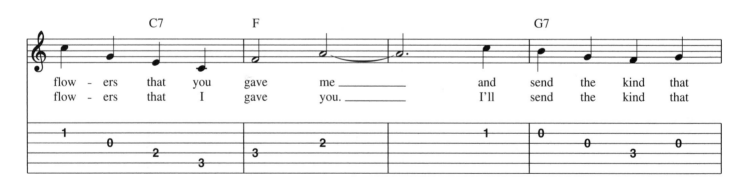

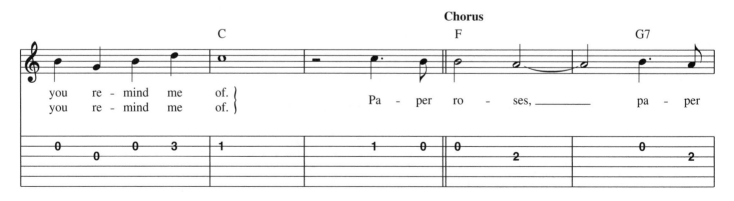

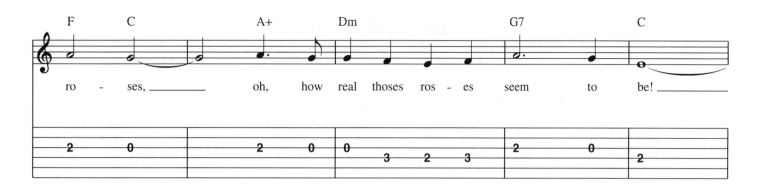

ro - ses, _____ oh, how real thoses ros - es seem to be! _____

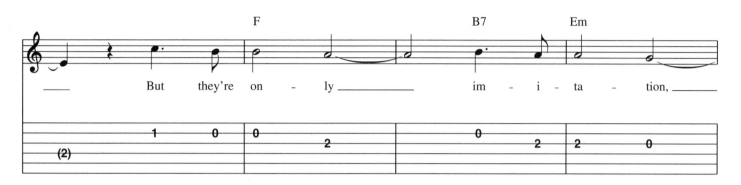

_____ But they're on - ly _____ im - i - ta - tion, _____

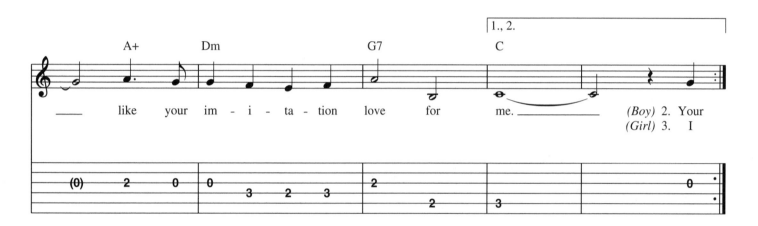

1., 2.

_____ like your im - i - ta - tion love for me. _____ *(Boy)* 2. Your
(Girl) 3. I

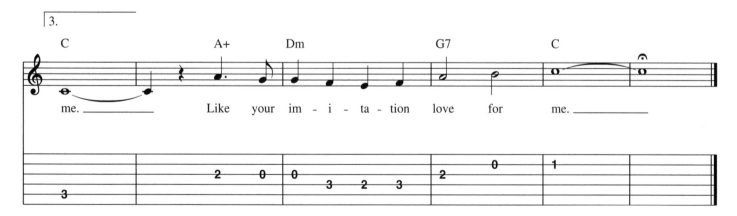

3.

me. _____ Like your im - i - ta - tion love for me. _____

Additional Lyrics

Boy 2. Your pretty lips look so warm and appealing;
They seem to have the sweetness of a rose;
But when you give a kiss there is no feeling;
It's just a still and artificial pose.

Girl 3. I thought that you would be a perfect lover,
You seemed so full of sweetness at the start.
But like a big red rose that's made out of paper,
There isn't any sweetness in your heart.

Release Me

Words and Music by Robert Yount, Eddie Miller and Dub Williams

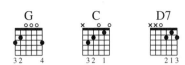

Strum Pattern: 3, 4
Pick Pattern: 3

Verse

Moderately slow

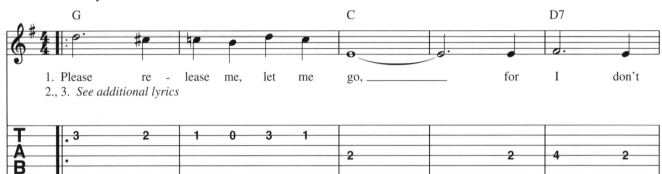

1. Please re - lease me, let me go, _____ for I don't
2., 3. *See additional lyrics*

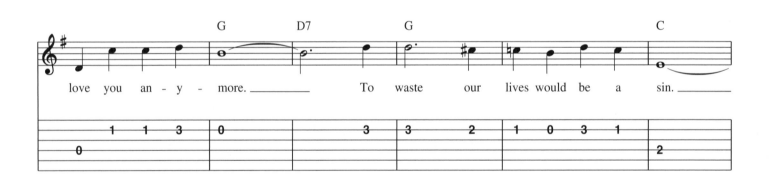

love you an - y - more. _____ To waste our lives would be a sin. _____

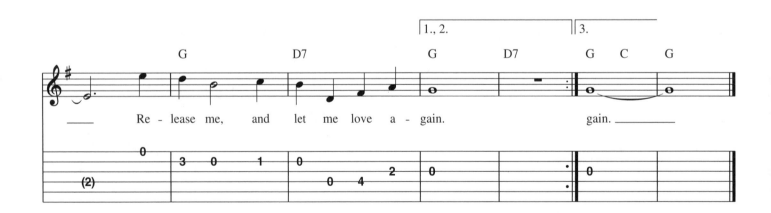

_____ Re - lease me, and let me love a - gain. gain. _____

Additional Lyrics

2. I have found a new love, dear,
   And I will always want her near.
   Her lips are warm while yours are cold.
   Release me, my darling, let me go.

3. Please release me, can't you see
   You'd be a fool to cling to me.
   To live a lie would be a pain.
   So release me, and let me love again.

Take Me Home, Country Roads

Words and Music by John Denver, Bill Danoff and Taffy Nivert

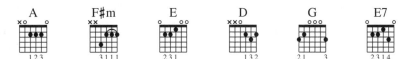

Strum Pattern: 3
Pick Pattern: 3

Verse

Bright Country

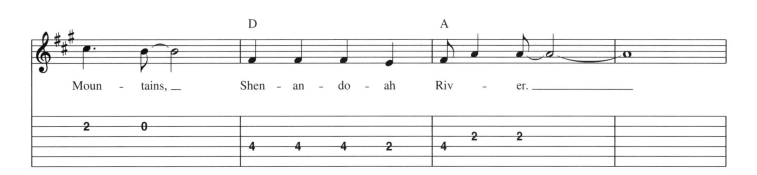

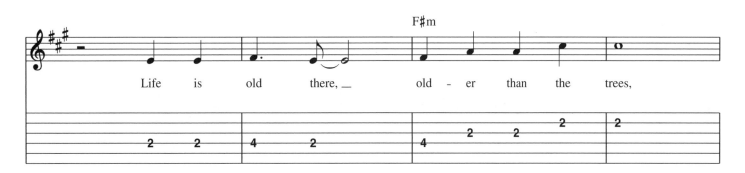

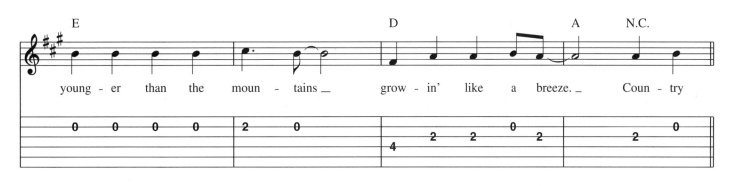

Additional Lyrics

2. All my mem'ries gather 'round her,
   Miner's lady, stranger to blue water.
   Dark and dusty, painted on the sky,
   Misty taste of moonshine, teardrop in my eye.

97

Rocky Mountain High

Words by John Denver

Music by John Denver and Mike Taylor

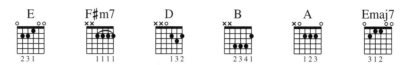

Strum Pattern: 1

Pick Pattern: 2

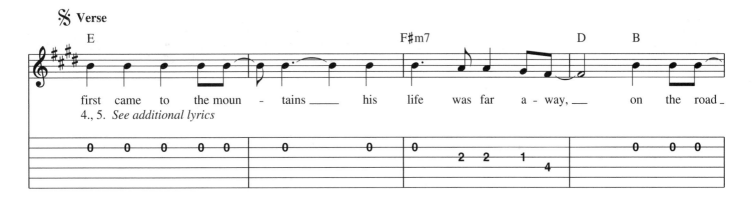

Verse

E   F#m7   D   B

first came to the moun - tains ___ his life was far a - way, ___ on the road ___
4., 5. *See additional lyrics*

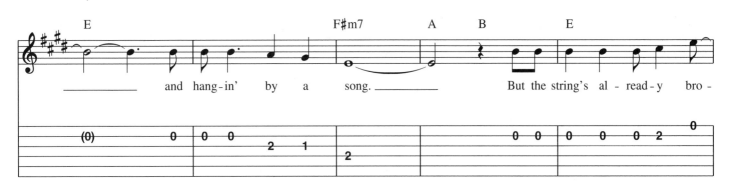

___ and hang - in' by a song. ___ But the string's al - read - y bro -

- ken and he does-n't real - ly care, ___ it keeps chang - in' fast ___ and

Chorus

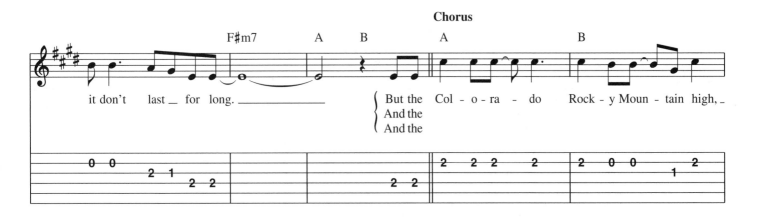

it don't last ___ for long. ___ But the Col - o - ra - do Rock - y Moun - tain high, ___
And the
And the

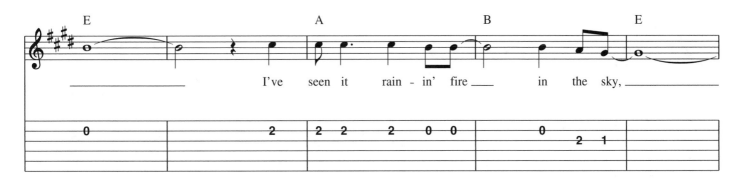

___ I've seen it rain - in' fire ___ in the sky, ___

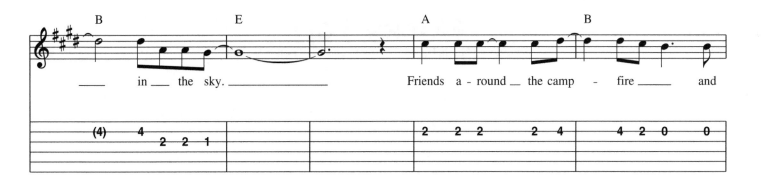

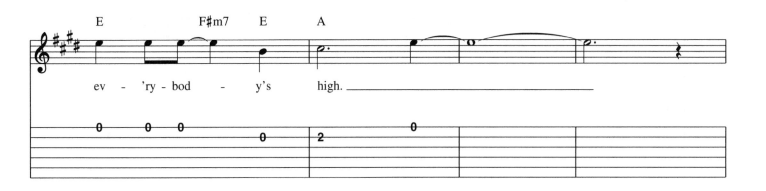

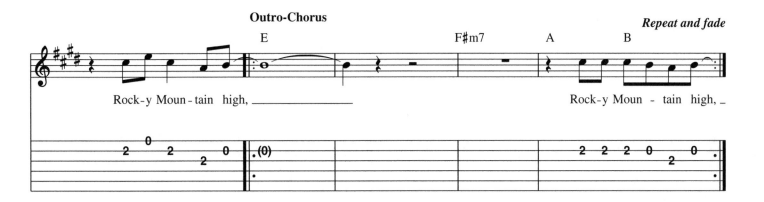

Additional Lyrics

3. He climbed Cathedral Mountains, he saw silver clouds below,
   He saw everything as far as you can see.
   And they say that he got crazy once and he tried to touch the sun,
   And he lost a friend but kept his memory.

4. Now he walks in quiet solitude, the forests and the streams
   Seeking grace in ev'ry step he takes.
   His sight has turned inside himself to try and understand
   The serenity of a clear blue mountain lake.

5. Now his life is full of wonder but his heart still knows some fear
   Of a simple thing he cannot comprehend.
   Why they try to tear the mountains down to bring in a couple more,
   More people, more scars upon the land.

Rocky Top

Words and Music by Boudleaux Bryant and Felice Bryant

Strum Pattern: 4
Pick Pattern: 5

Verse

Lively

1. Wish that I was on ol' Rock-y Top down in the Ten-nes-see hills.
3. *See additional lyrics*

Ain't no smog-gy smoke on Rock-y Top, ain't no tel-e-phone __ bills.

Verse

2. Once I had a girl on Rock-y Top half bear the oth-er half cat.
4., 5. *See additional lyrics*

Wild as a mink, but sweet as so-da pop I still dream a-bout that.

Chorus

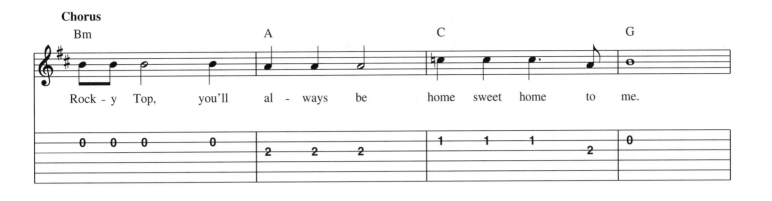

Rock - y Top, you'll al - ways be home sweet home to me.

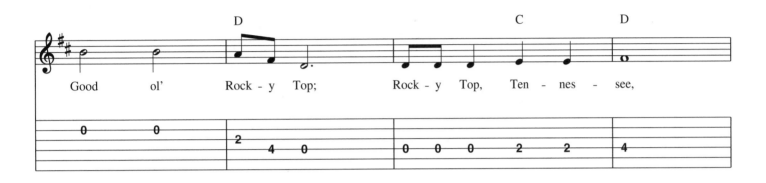

Good ol' Rock - y Top; Rock - y Top, Ten - nes - see,

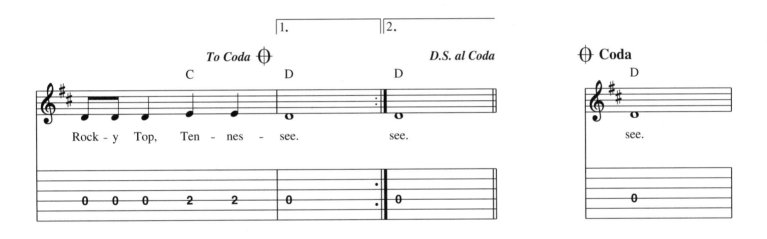

Rock - y Top, Ten - nes - see. see. see.

To Coda ⊕ *D.S. al Coda* ⊕ **Coda**

|1. |2.

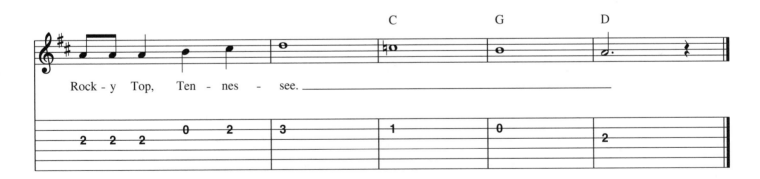

Rock - y Top, Ten - nes - see. _____

Additional Lyrics

3. Once two strangers climbed ol' Rocky Top, lookin' for a moonshine still.
   Strangers ain't come down from Rocky Top, reckon they never will.

4. Corn won't grow at all on Rocky Top, dirt's too rocky by far.
   That's why all the folks on Rocky Top get their corn from a jar.

5. I've had years of cramped-up life, trapped like a duck in a pen.
   All I know is it's a pity life can't be simple again.

Sixteen Tons

Words and Music by Merle Travis

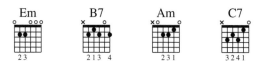

Strum Pattern: 3, 6
Pick Pattern: 5, 6

Intro
Moderately

1. Some

Verse

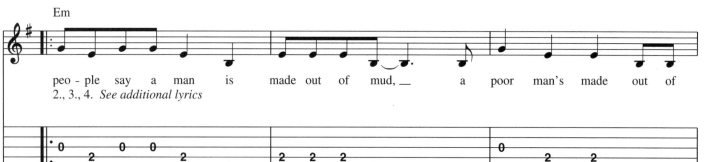

peo- ple say a man is made out of mud, ___ a poor man's made out of
2., 3., 4. *See additional lyrics*

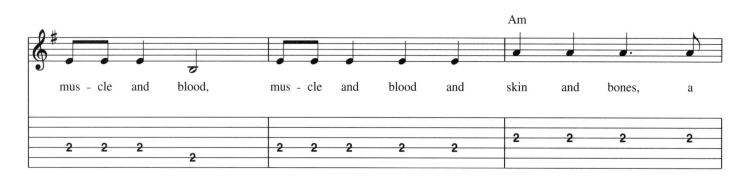

mus- cle and blood, mus- cle and blood and skin and bones, a

Chorus

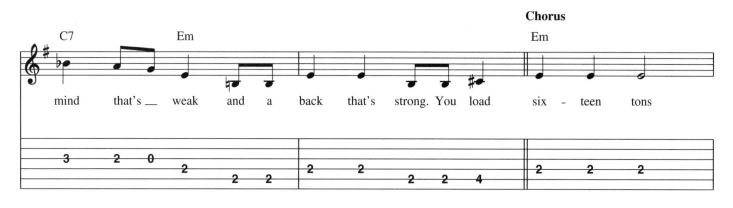

mind that's ___ weak and a back that's strong. You load six - teen tons

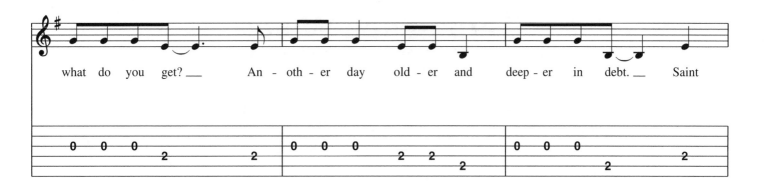

what do you get? __ An - oth - er day old - er and deep - er in debt. __ Saint

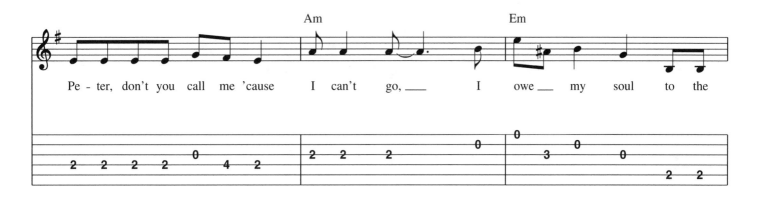

Pe - ter, don't you call me 'cause I can't go, __ I owe __ my soul to the

1., 2., 3.   4.

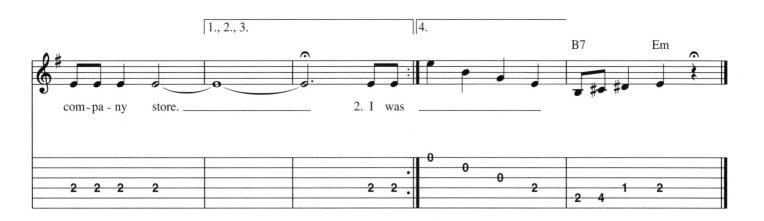

com - pa - ny store. _____ 2. I was _____

Additional Lyrics

2. I was born one mornin' when the sun didn't shine.
   I picked up my shovel and I walked to the mine.
   I loaded sixteen tons of number nine coal,
   And the strawboss said, "Wella bless my soul."

3. I was born one mornin', it was drizzling rain.
   Fightin' and trouble are my middle name.
   I was raised in a canebreak by an ole mama lion.
   Cain't no hightoned woman make me walk the line.

4. If you see me comin' better step aside,
   A lotta men didn't a lotta men died.
   One fist of iron the other of steel,
   If the right one don't-a get you, then the left one will.

Tennessee Waltz

Words and Music by Redd Stewart and Pee Wee King

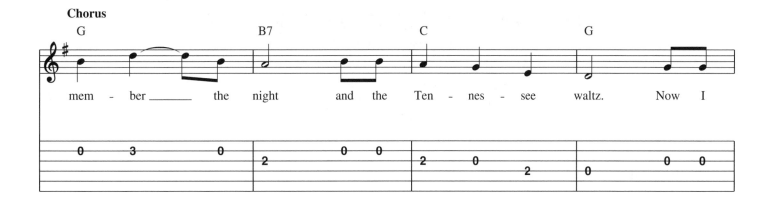

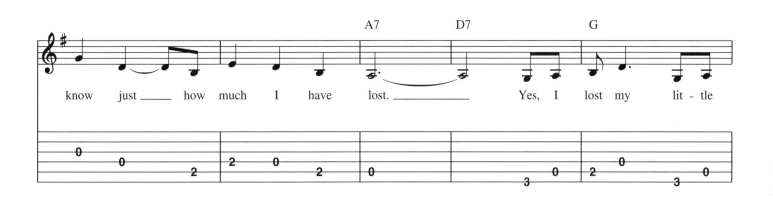

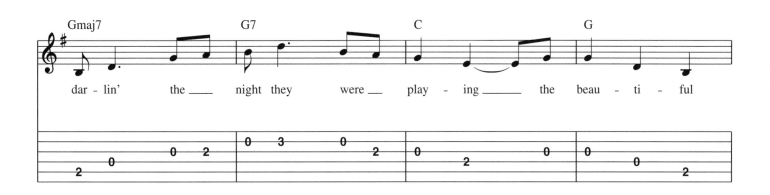

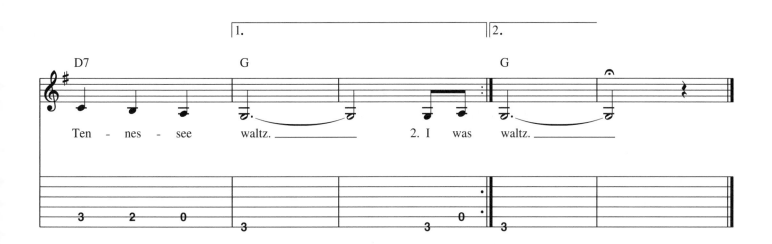

There's a Tear in My Beer

Words and Music by Hank Williams

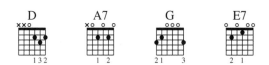

Strum Pattern: 4
Pick Pattern: 3

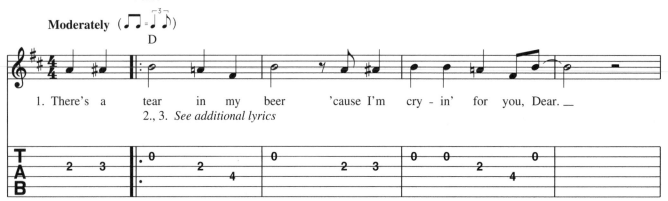

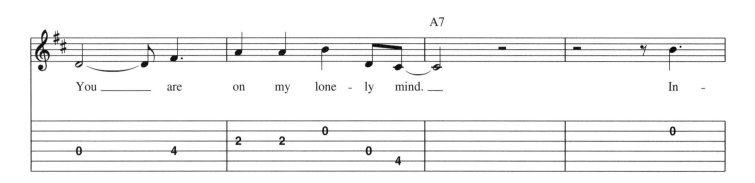

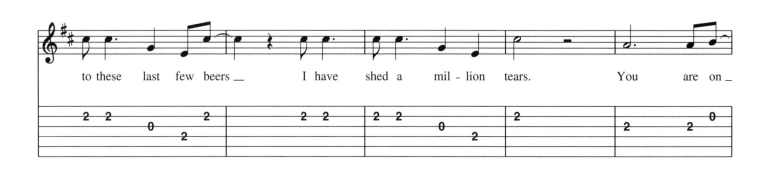

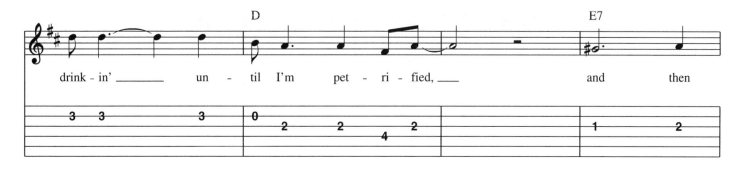

drink - in' _____ un - til I'm pet - ri - fied, ____ and then

may - be these tears ___ will leave _ my eyes. ___ There's a tear ___ in my beer _

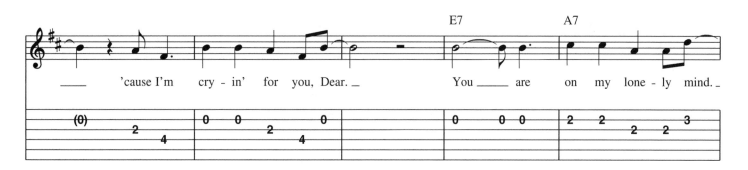

____ 'cause I'm cry - in' for you, Dear. _ You _____ are on my lone - ly mind. _

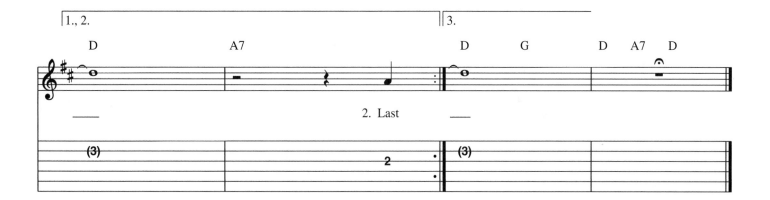

1., 2.   3.

D   A7   D   G   D   A7   D

____   2. Last   ____

Additional Lyrics

2. Last night I walked the floor and the night before;
   You are on my lonely mind.
   It seems my life is through and I'm so dog-gone blue.
   You are on my lonely mind.
   I'm gonna keep drinkin' till I can't move a toe,
   And then maybe my heart won't hurt me so.
   There's a tear in my beer 'cause I'm crying for you, Dear.
   You are on my lonely mind.

3. Lord, I've tried, and I've tried but my tears I can't hide;
   You are on my lonely mind.
   All these blues that I've found have really got me down.
   You were on my lonely mind.
   I'm gonna keep drinkin' till I can't even think,
   'Cause in the last week, I ain't slep' a wink.
   There's a tear in my beer 'cause I'm crying for you, Dear.
   You were on my lonely mind.

Walkin' After Midnight

Lyrics by Don Hecht
Music by Alan W. Block

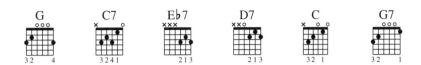

Strum Pattern: 1
Pick Pattern: 2

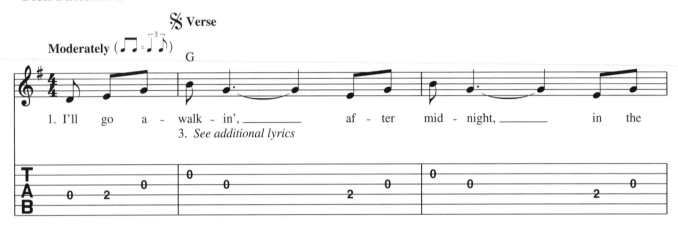

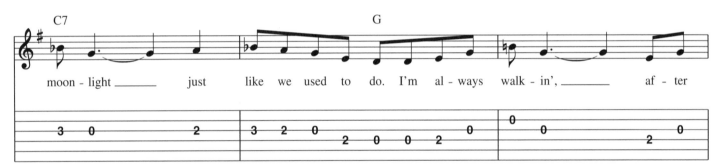

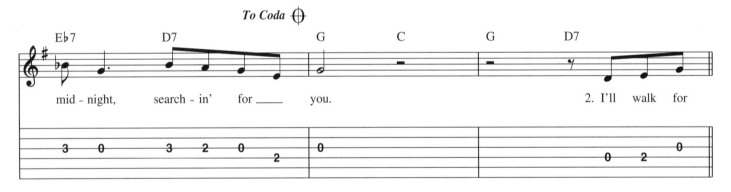

Additional Lyrics

3. I'll go out walkin', after midnight,
   In the starlight, and pray that you may be
   Somewhere just walkin' after midnight,
   Searchin' for me.

When Will I Be Loved

Words and Music by Phil Everly

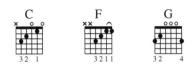

Strum Pattern: 1
Pick Pattern: 2

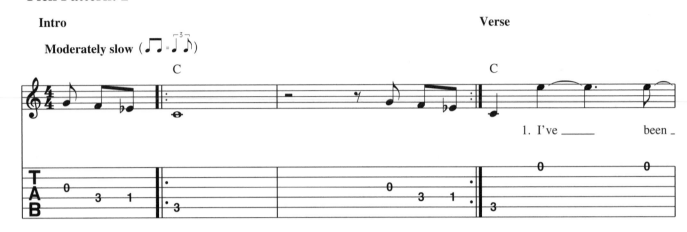

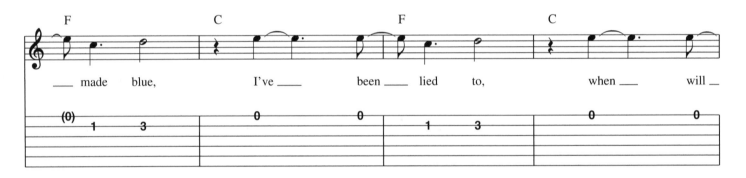

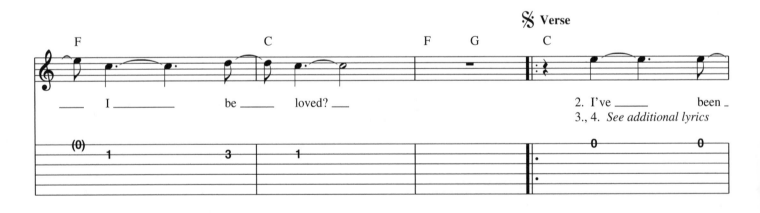

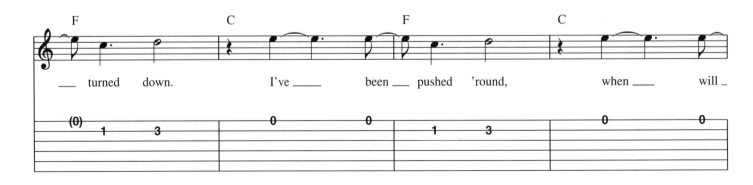

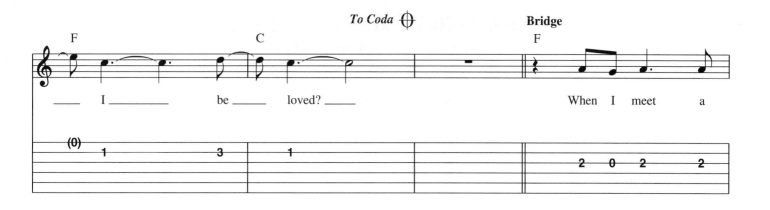

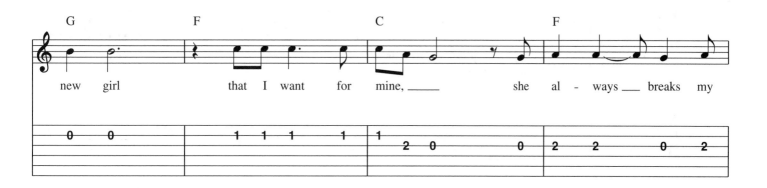

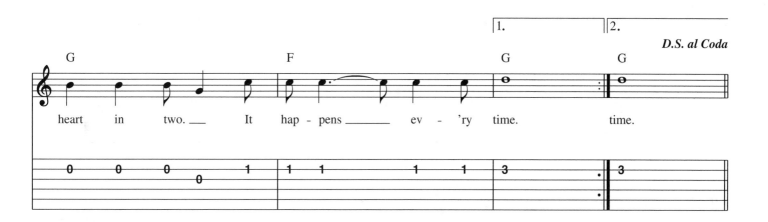

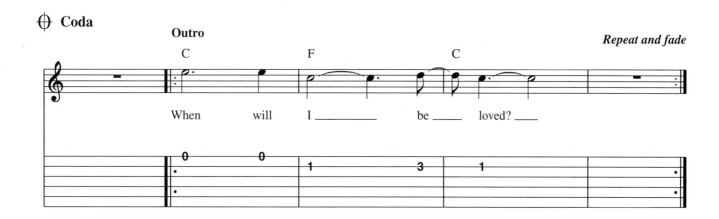

Additional Lyrics

3., 4. I've been cheated,
Been mistreated,
When will I be loved?

Workin' Man Blues

Words and Music by Merle Haggard

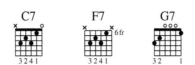

Strum Pattern: 6
Pick Pattern: 4

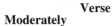

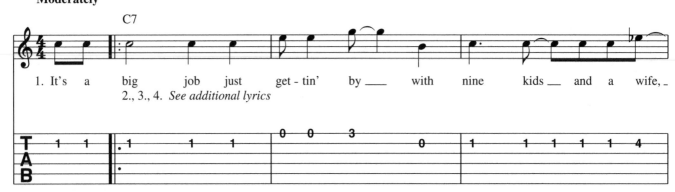

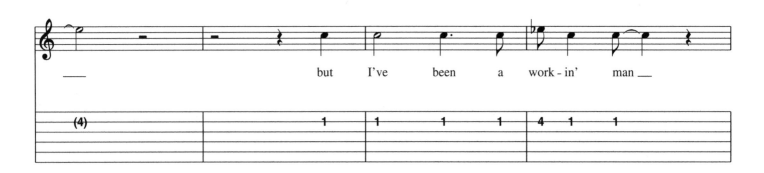

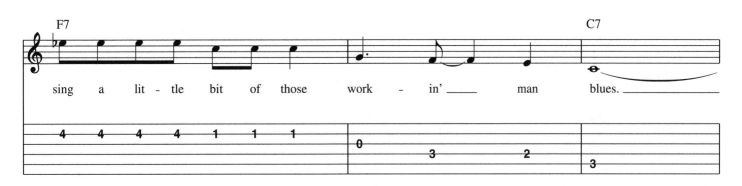

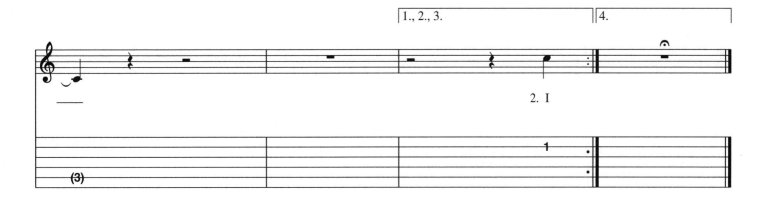

Additional Lyrics

2. I keep my nose on the grindstone, work hard every day.
   I might get a little tired on the weekend, after I draw my pay,
   I'll go back workin', come Monday morning I'm right back with the crew.
   I drink a little beer that evening,
   Sing a little bit of these workin' man blues.

3. Sometimes I think about leaving, do a little bumming around.
   I want to throw my bills out the window, catch a train to another town.
   I'll go back workin', gotta buy my kids a brand new pair of shoes.
   I drink a little beer in a tavern,
   Cry a little bit of these workin' man blues.

4. Well, hey! Hey! The working man, the workin' man like me;
   I ain't never been on welfare, that's one place I won't be.
   I'll be workin', long as my two hands are fit to use.
   I drink a little beer in a tavern,
   Sing a little bit of these workin' man blues.

Your Cheatin' Heart

Words and Music by Hank Williams

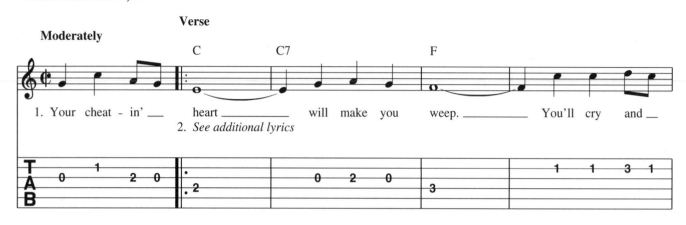

Strum Pattern: 3, 2
Pick Pattern: 3, 6

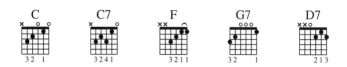

Verse

Moderately

1. Your cheat - in' ___ heart ___ will make you weep. ___ You'll cry and ___

2. *See additional lyrics*

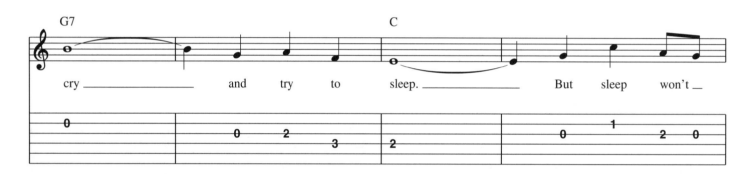

cry ___ and try to sleep. ___ But sleep won't ___

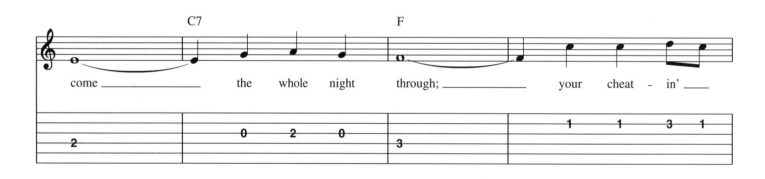

come ___ the whole night through; ___ your cheat - in' ___

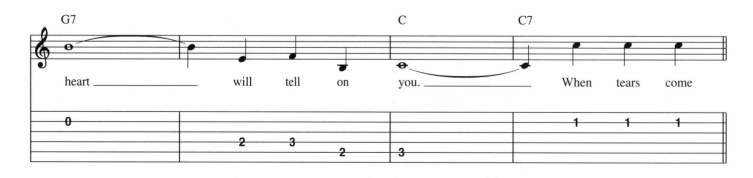

heart ___ will tell on you. ___ When tears come

Bridge

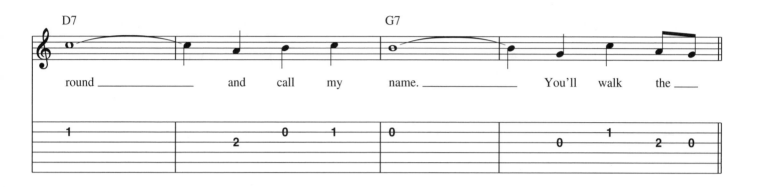

Outro

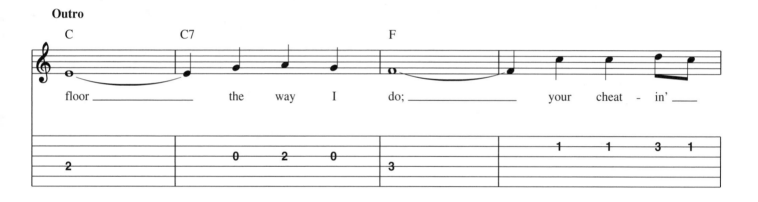

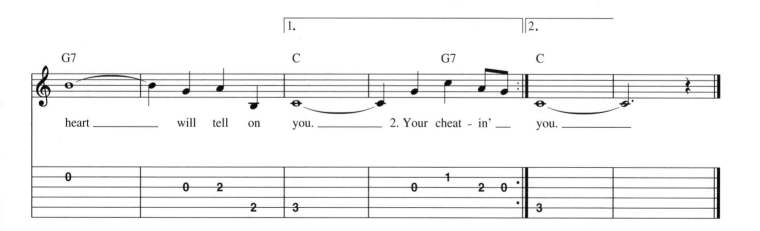

Additional Lyrics

2. Your cheatin' heart will pine someday,
And crave the love you threw away.
The time will come when you'll be blue.
Your cheatin' heart will tell on you.

You're the Reason God Made Oklahoma

Words and Music by Sandy Pinkard, Larry Collins, Boudleaux Bryant and Felice Bryant

Strum Pattern: 1
Pick Pattern: 4

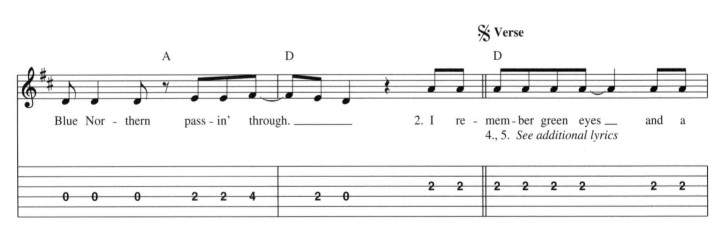

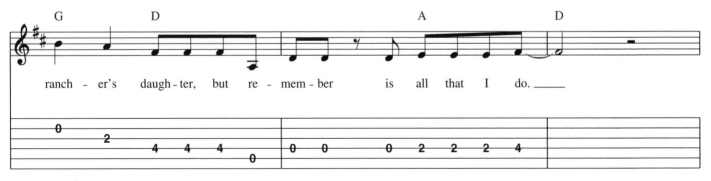

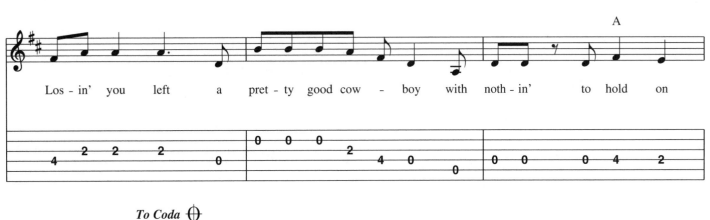

Los - in' you left a pret - ty good cow - boy with noth - in' to hold on to.

To Coda ⊕ **Bridge**

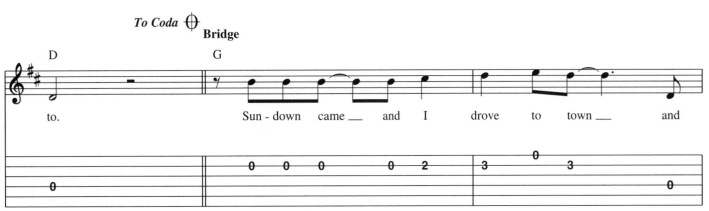

Sun - down came __ and I drove to town __ and

Chorus

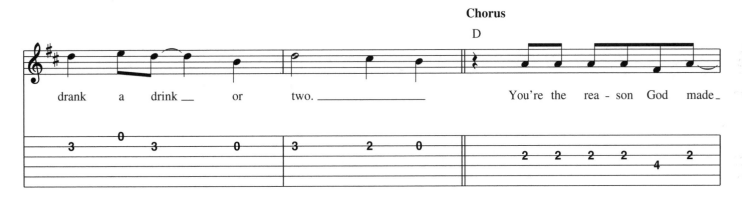

drank a drink __ or two. _____ You're the rea - son God made __

__ Ok - la - ho - ma. You're the rea - son God made __ Ok - la - ho - ma, and

1.

I'm sure mis - sin' you. _____ And I'm sure mis - sin'

⊕ Coda

Chorus

You're the rea - son God made ___ Ok - la - ho - ma.

You're the rea - son God made ___ Ok - la - ho - ma, and I'm sure mis - sin'

you. ___ And I'm sure mis - sin' you.

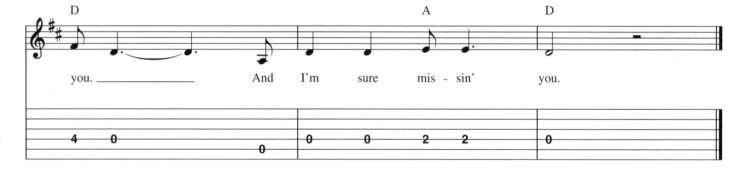

Additional Lyrics

3. Here, the city lights outshine the moon.
   I was just now thinking of you.
   Sometimes when the wind blows you can see the mountains
   And all the way to Malibu.

4. Ev'ryone's a star here in L.A. County.
   You ought to see the things that they do.
   All the cowboys down on the Sunset Strip
   Wish that they could be like you,
   The Santa Monica Freeway sometimes makes a country girl blue.

5. I worked ten hours on a John Deere tractor
   Just thinkin' of you all day.
   I've got a calico cat and a two room flat
   On a street in West L.A.